PN Review 245

VOLUME 45   NUMBER 3   JANUARY – FEBRUA

SOME CONTRIBUTORS

Tamar Yoseloff's sixth collection, *The Black Place*, will be published by Seren in 2019. She is currently a lecturer on the Newcastle University/Poetry School MA in Writing Poetry. **Les Murray** was born in 1938, and lives on the North Coast of New South Wales. He has been described as Australia's greatest writer, in any genre. **Lesley Harrison** lives and works on the northern coastline. Her most recent collection is *Blue Pearl* (New Directions). A full collection is due out shortly. **Michael Krüger**, poet, novelist, translator and editor, was born in Saxony in 1943 and was presented the Lifetime Achievement Award in International Publishing by the London Book Fair. His most recent collection of poetry is *Einmal einfach* (2018). **Patrick McGuinness**'s new novel is *Throw me to the Wolves*.

ON THE COVER: Humphrey Ocean, 'Traffic', courtesy of the artist. *Photograph:* Mike Bruce

Editorial

Some get grumpy about this new diversity of platforms and voices, as they are used to a certain type of poetry being held up as best; to narrow definitions of 'craft' and 'seriousness'. It's like they love wine so have spent a lifetime memorising the subtleties of certain grapes, vintages, *terroir*, and suddenly they're being offered a coffee, a cocktail or a smoothie. 'But this isn't a Rioja!' they bellow. Well, I like wine as well, but not all the time, and, once you educate yourself, you discover there can be as much skill involved in the preparation of other drinks. Let's raise a cup of whatever you enjoy to the current state of poetry!

— CLARE POLLARD

ON 22 NOVEMBER Sandeep Parmar contributed to the *Guardian* a provocative think piece. It was shared over 1,200 times on the first day. She was answering Rose Tremain and Robin Robertson, both of whom had spoken disobligingly about contemporary poetry. Tremain told the *TLS*, 'Let's dare to say it out loud: contemporary poetry is in a rotten state. [...] Having binned all the rules, most poets seem to think that rolling out some pastry-coloured prose, adding a sprinkling of white space, then cutting it up into little shapelets will do.' The Big Bake Off language does not amuse Parmar. Overlooking the word 'contemporary', she has Tremain reject a century and a half's poetry, having 'leapt over the cross-currents of the next 100 years from Tennyson to Walter de la Mare to Philip Larkin, flat-footing it on their bald, smooth verse to land on some plaintive lyrical bank of our new century'. But she hadn't. 'Bald' is slyly gendered, and to reduce the diverse prosodies of Larkin, de la Mare and Tennyson to 'flat-footing' suggests an aural malfunction that needs attention.

'Detractors of new poetry make judgments about craft based on conservative assumptions about poetic traditions, forms, style,' she says, but 'radical aesthetics have their own craft and traditions, formed from intersecting political and linguistic concerns.' Very well, what are those crafts and traditions? 'So this isn't a question of craft at all,' she non-seqs.

In an interview Robin Robertson said contemporary poetry divides into 'light verse' at one extreme and 'incomprehensible' verse at the other. Parmar portrays him sitting 'somewhere in the appalled middle, frustrated by poets seeking "likes" on social media, "driven by self-promotion and shallow narcissism", who haven't the time "to bother with all that pesky learning-the-craft business".' She asks for names. Certainly Robertson's would strengthen his case with detail. So could she.

She recounts her experience, participating in a National Poetry Day event entitled PoetryInquisition, 'which sprang from Jeremy Paxman's statement as a Forward Prize judge in 2014 that poets should be publicly held to account because, in speaking only to each other, their art had "connived at its own irrelevance".' A questioner from the floor 'began [...] by quoting Robertson's interview to support his own attack on identity politics in poetry'. When she asked him to define 'identity-based poetry' he 'unleashed a misogynist and racist tirade, and was finally heckled quiet by the assembled crowd'. She tells us, 'identity-based poetry' is not solely the preserve of the 'marginalised'. It covers white, middle-class men, too. 'Indeed, *they* have been writing identity-based poetry for centuries.'

'We need to have a meaningful discussion about the value of our changing poetry culture,' she concludes, 'one that is open to many voices as well as rigorous and critical. But most of all, it needs to be honest.' I asked the *Guardian* if I might respond. There was no space.

Reading Parmar's piece and other less nuanced polemics, I see how easily clichés that ensnare and silence whole categories of individual can take shape. And how they must be resisted. As a white male in the vale of years with what used to be regarded as a good education and years of service on Parnassus, I become anathematised. I am not welcome in various fora because of what rather than who I am. 'You would say that, wouldn't you', the heckler says, silencing me.

When Parmar talks about the aesthetics of newness and conjures Audre Lorde in 1977, Levertov in 1965, and Creeley and Olson, with their debts to Williams, Pound, Whitman, she's far from new. And these poets each had long, diverse trajectories and cannot be impaled on the pin of Vietnam or McCarthyism or breath theory or variable foot. There are aesthetics of newness in Hopkins, Pound, Eliot, Moore, Rosenberg, Mew, and in the women modernists of whom Parmar is a key scholar and a subtle champion. But they are not new now.

To include swathes of work emerging now in the same sentence with such linguistically and formally diverse and radical work by individuals, their revolutions in *craft* (the term valuable still in composing and assessing poetry), is to misvalue the past and the present. When the appreciation of an art form is politicised, the rhetoric has consequences for readers and for writers themselves. The quality of critical engagement (the culture of reception) affects creative culture. Enrichment comes to poetry from the many different Englishes, a diversity threatened when 'identity politics' insists that poets must speak not only from but also of their lived experience, in terms calibrated to conform to the politicised aesthetics of the day. The rejection of craft can be enabling if poets know how to do it and why they are discarding it. To discard something because it is too difficult is another matter. In poetry, otherness earns its spurs *as poetry*, sometimes against ingrained resistance and prejudice. Whitman inventing the American line is a paradigm of earned mastery, writing through to his subjects and his forms. Adrienne Rich diving into the wreck is another.

If you ask for wine and are brought a smoothie, you have a right to be disappointed.

Cover Story

Humphrey Ocean, 'Traffic'

IT IS A STRIKING PARADOX that Humphrey Ocean, so well known as a portraitist, should have painted so many scenes without figures: the more so, because they often include studies of British domestic architecture or suburban infrastructure. Where are all the bodies? It is not that these scenes are empty of humanity, simply that the people are all hidden. In 'Traffic', the emblematic white van has hit the road, in a world that is nearly all tarmac, with the evidence of nature nearly all squeezed into the verge. This is not a representation of observable reality as much as a proportional emphasis on what is conceptually important in today's Britain, a place where the priority is to find ever more space for the white van man to move into. Ocean's technique might be thought of as proportional realism. His street lights glowing in the daytime conform to the view that everything natural is redundant. But nature fights back, in our inherited way of seeing it, and that depends above all on the example of art. Suburban streets and the lives passed within them are so well known that we do not think about them or even look at them anymore. And it is precisely in this zone of the over familiar that Ocean finds the biggest story of all: this is the world that we have made, the one that represents us – this is the true mirror of our times.

Rod Mengham

Letters to the Editor

IAIN BAMFORTH *writes* · Your most recent editorial relating Christian Wiman's recollections of his American poet colleagues in 'He Held Radical Light' had me thinking. Like so many poets I too have stared the prospect of radical failure in the face, and of course felt just like A.R. Ammons at his poetry reading, although never sat down in the middle of one having just announced to a cluster of incredulous listeners that the reading was going to stop right there and then. Jacques Derrida might have suggested that Ammons had failed to turn up in his own poems, to be sufficiently *present*. Whatever original intentionality they possessed was now lost in the illocutionary act, and were ashes in his mouth. Perhaps other, parasitic factors were at work. One of Derrida's sources, the analytic philosopher J.L. Austin, put in these terms: 'as *utterances* our performances are also heir to certain other kinds of ill which affect *all* utterances'.

Yet Ammons clearly never felt disgusted enough with being a scriptor – a poet committing words to the page as opposed to a lector, or reciter of his works – to give up being a poet: he went on writing until his death in 2001, and the Ammons' poems I know, curiously enough, don't seem to object to leaving a scientific lexis (geology, botany) in the keeping of the ordinary demotic. It may be that he needed the paradoxes of the written form, as in Plato's *Phaedrus*, which is an indictment in writing of writing itself, to convince himself that he could get poems down on paper, and repeat the act. And do it without any *determinate* person in mind. Osip Mandelstam (whose work Wiman has translated) explains how it's done, in his essay 'Concerning the addressee' (1913): 'Poetry taken as a whole is always sent to an addressee who is more or less remote and unknown, an addressee whose real existence the poet cannot doubt, lest he doubt himself.'

LETTER TO THE EDITORS OF THE *GUARDIAN* WHICH THEY DECLINED TO PUBLISH · Dear Editors, Simon Armitage writes [in the *Guardian*, 2 November] about the role of the Poet to represent these islands' traditions as someone who is 'admired by both their fellow poets and by the public.' But Richard Lea's report outlines the government's advisory committee which Minister Jeremy Wright says 'reflects the whole of the UK and the new ways we consume poetry'.

Readers do not have to be especially perceptive, however, to observe that no writers are part of the process. Arts Council leads, festival and competition promoters and arts CEOs, yes but no writers, and in particular none of the 'fellow poets' Armitage values.

Not one member of the committee identifies as a poet or as a poetry critic and, perhaps predictably from a government whose members have derided expert opinion, there is no member recruited from any of the many universities which research and teach courses on poetry.

Maybe the next Laureate will fit the description Armitage proposes, but if so it will be doing so by guesswork, and it is just as likely these advisors will, in spite of best intentions, skew the decision-making away from the art of making poems.

This selection process depends too heavily on the opinions of arts professionals, many without expertise on poetry, and should be revised so as to involve working writers · JOHN MCAULIFFE, Professor of Modern Literature and Creative Writing, Co-director, Centre for New Writing, University of Manchester

News & Notes

Three Crowns · *John Clegg* writes: On Saturday 15 September there was a well-attended service at St James, Piccadilly, marking the centenary of John Heath-Stubbs's birth. Among the readers, Eddie Linden gave a particularly memorable performance of 'A Crow in Bayswater'. There was also a rare performance of three songs from *The Unicorns*, John's abortive libretto, commissioned and set by Peter Dickinson and sung by Susanna Fairborn. The attendees subsequently adjoined to the Three Crowns to drink John's health.

Open Access · With the rapid advance of academic publishing towards Open Access, the erosion of copyright, which protects the creative rights of inventors of and through language, is coming under cruder and harsher compulsions in certain parliaments. The Copyright Amendment Bill introduced in the South African National Assembly will be debated and voted on in its Second Reading. It was introduced in May 2017. Amendments to the 1978 Act were intended to accommodate digital era and 'improve protection of artists and authors'. The new Bill 'is poorly drafted and not based on clear policy'. Industry and legal experts say it cannot be implemented and breaches many international treaty obligations. It allows the use of copyright materials without permission and therefore without compensation to copyright holders – authors, illustrators and publishers. Entire books can be 'copied for 'educational purposes' in certain circumstances'. Authors and publishers are left without recourse. The losses to publishing are estimated at R2.1 billion a year. A number of organisations, including PEN South Africa, PEN Afrikaans, the Association for Academic and Nonfiction Authors of South Africa (ANFASA), PASA and others have joined in continued protest by means of a petition (facilitated by LitNet). The link to the petition is here: https://www.litnet.co.za/south-african-authors-protest-against-copyright-amendment-bill/.

Impossible Grace · *Yogesh Patel writes*: Meena Alexander's poem published in the *New Yorker* in the aftermath of 9/11 was 'Kabir Sings in a City of Burning Towers'. Kabir was a weaver, born into a Muslim family, who practised Hinduism. He was a critic of both. 'What a shame / they scared you so / you plucked your sari off, / crushed it into a ball // Then spread it / on the toilet floor. / Sparks from the towers / fled through the weaves of silk.' This sense of perils, survivals, fusions, marks her poetry. She died in November at the age of sixty-seven, after a long stand-off with cancer. On her last visit to London she collected the Word Masala Award in the House of Lords. A grand poet, a Distinguished Professor of English at Hunter College, the City University of New York, she was loved and respected internationally as a writer and scholar. We had a strong bond through Umashankar Joshi, winner of India's national Jnanpith Award. He was an 'elder' friend to me but 'Bapuji' (a father figure) to her. She never avoided the hard themes. She wrote in Jerusalem: 'At Golden gate, / Where rooftops ring with music, / I glimpse your face. / You have a coat of many colours – impossible grace.'

Born into a Syrian Christian family in India, her formative years from the age of five were spent in Sudan where she took her BA at the University of Khartoum. Though she was in Britain earning her PhD at Nottingham, she went to India to teach. Finally, America claimed her.

On the deck of Karanja from Africa to India, I too experienced the sense of being nowhere. Meena's poems often speak from that deck. She borrowed a green coat from Celan for – as her recent writing indicates – she was troubled with 'a world of nationalism gone awry' as she wrote recently: 'We have no words/for what is happening – // Still language endures / Celan said // As he stood in a torn / Green coat // Shivering a little, / In a night theatre, in Bremen.'

Lopamudra Basu and Cynthia Leenerts suggest that Meena Alexander created 'a new hybrid poetic form, which fuses the Western Romantic lyric tradition with non-Western ones of Bhakti and Sufi poetry' from India. Keki Daruwalla reflected on her work: 'Her output is phenomenal — memoir, scholarship, her writings on identity. She wrote on political subjects too, all that happened on the political stage was close to her heart. [...] In Indian poetry in English, we have had Kamala Das and Eunice de Souza, Arundhati Subramaniam is well on her way to join them, and Meena is certainly there.'

Mixing slapstick and surrealism · The poet Judith Kazantzis died in September at the age of seventy-eight. She published a dozen collections, and essays and a novel. Some of her early poems develop and reinvent the roles of women in legend and fairytale, complementing what other writers were doing in prose. Her Clytemnestra, she declared, was not 'a crazy bitch', but 'a human being with strong passions and good reasons'. Her later poems made emphatic political statements relating to current affairs, sometimes polemical, sometimes elegiac. Evoking the variety of her work, the *Guardian* obituarist wrote, 'In *Sister Invention* (2014), the poems sneak up on both the powerful and the weak, eavesdropping, spying, reporting back to the reader in intimate, deadpan tones, mixing slapstick and surrealism to convey the horrors of hi-tech warfare. Yet in this same volume Judith's imagination also encompasses journeys around North American landscapes, pilgrimages across the terrain of family and of love.'

High priest of irony · The poet Tony Hoagland died of cancer in October at the age of sixty-four. His publishers at Bloodaxe wrote: 'A provocative poet, critic and literary figure, he was American poetry's hilarious 'high priest of irony', a wisecracker and a risk-taker whose disarming humour, self-scathing and tenderness were all fuelled by an aggressive moral intelligence. His poems poke and provoke at the same time as they entertain and delight. He pushed the poem not just to its limits but over the edge.' He published three books of poetry with Bloodaxe, with a fourth due out in 2019. British audiences first encountered him at the Aldeburgh Poetry Festival in 2004. He was a popular poet-in-residence at Ledbury Poetry Festival in 2017, lecturing on the American poetic voice and giving poetry workshops.

B.C. · *Martin Elliott sent us this appreciation of B.C. Leale (1930–2018).* He was a member of 'The Group', which met in Chelsea to read and criticise one another's verse in the late 1950s and early '60s. His work appeared in major weeklies and in small magazines, for example *Ambit, Bang, Pink Peace* and *Slow Dancer* – some fifty periodical outlets in all (though not *PN Review*.) Several anthologies also featured his work. Barry Cavendish Leale – always B.C. in print – had a first collection, *Leviathan* published by Allison and Busby in 1984. It was a Poetry Book Society Recommendation. Later in that year, John Calder published his surrealist poems as *The Colours of Ancient Dreams*. 'Surrealismo' would be a more accurate account of the later work, since It describes and celebrates the early-century worlds of Paris and Lucerne and is haunted by Bréton, Duchamp, Magritte. Even when the modern world is addressed, it's usually through the illogic of Barry's own fin de siècle dreams. The older epoch is rarely far away. I'd suggest Barry was at his unique and considerable best when suggesting human or animal presences through images or the workings of art. So: 'You laugh / you jump up & / down in green-brown / rhythmic brush-strokes' (Frognal Way, Hampstead). Similarly, the dog in Sketch by Constable 'knows it's an early draft. He's / full of destinations and joy as he / rounds the first bend from the house. . .'

The verse overall is intense, powerful, with a never-failing sense of fun. Many titles demand that a poem be read – viz, 'Our Baroque Cat', 'To savour the lake', 'Aunts in a deep sleep'... Writing less as he aged, Barry sent out no submissions in his latter years. His literary executors are considering how best to deploy the large store of his later poems.

In that rickety fashion · *Yogesh Patel writes*: Anthony Rudolf's note in *PNR* 244 triggered some reminiscence of our work at the magazine *Skylark*, neglected now. Like Menard Press, we published our first issue, from Aligarh, in 1969. Our aim was to publish poetry in translation from around the world and from the regional languages of India, and to include emerging poets from the English literature in India. We ran to one hundred issues at a time before email, battling with stamps, the typical Indian problem of currency conversion, the packing requirements of the postal service, the queues at lazy post offices, and no intercity telephone lines.

Skylark was founded by the late Baldev Mirza. A student of optometry at the state medical faculty, I joined Baldev as co-editor in 1969. We set up letterpress printing in an Aligarh slum to meet our budget. *Skylark* continued to print in that rickety fashion until its final issue. Then it slipped into obscurity. Such labour-intensive printing would never do now. Baldev has died and many issues of Skylark are lost. I have a few random issues. But with the postcolonial Indian English literature only in its second decade, the magazine had a profound influence. New voices had a podium where they stood alongside inter-national poets in translation. I revisited *Skylark*'s surviving issues and a note from Terry Cuthbert in Oxford fell out of one: 'Wazir Agha (Pakistan) is very much an excellent poet & you must be proud of getting his work in your magazine. You seem to be an important cultural event in India, and I know that many in your sub-continent love poetry, which is more than can be said with the average Englishman!'

Poets from Korea, Italy, New Zealand, Australia, Austria, UK, USA, Canada, China, Bosnia, Argentina, Germany, Arabic region, Pakistan, Bangladesh, Sri Lanka, Russia, Japan, Israel, Norway, Chile, Hungary, and more countries worked with us. We published Borges, Neruda, Amichai, Tsutomu Fukuda, Carlo Copolla, Wazir Agha, Shivkumar Batalvi, Amrita Pritam, Niranjan Mohanty, Jayant Mahapatra, Kamala Dash, O.P. Bhatnagar, and other great and unknown poets, despite the punishing printing and postal drudgeries. *Skylark* did well with special issues, bought in bulk by the certain embassies, and this inspired our special number on the diplomat poets.

We listened and innocently acted on subscribers' suggestions. In one of our unique issues, we curated poems from German writers who went into exile during the Second World War. We first published a special American women's poetry number. We never dated our issues, so now I am unable to recall when this fifty-second issue appeared.

To further our struggle against discrimination, we dared to publish a Dalit poetry issue. There were others too: Poems from Bosnia and Herzegovina, and Austrian poetry. We managed to publish a handful of pamphlets. *Skylark* UK, which I established, still helps Indian diaspora poetry. Nostalgia is a good place but perhaps it is time to hang up my hat as my friend Tony has! 'The road that was my companion / disappears ahead / leaving me stranded here...' (Raghuveer Chaudhary, Jnanpith Award Winner, translated from Gujarati by me).

Syntax Poems

Making Multivocal Performance Texts

VAHNI CAPILDEO

The writer Martin Carter (1927–1997) was involved in the conscious creation of Guyana, from revolutionary times and his jail writings to his representative later roles, from government minister to beloved regional poet. He was sensitive to the histories inscribed in his, and any, land as 'tongueless whispering'. Today's Caribbean is no less animated and inscribed by the 'shape and motion' of Carter's language. His original audiences could recite his poems by heart. Nowadays his words continue to make their way into genuinely popular song, protest and performance, for example during the curfew-challenging event in Trinidad in 2011, 'I Dream to Change the World'.

Why then my transreading of Carter to produce new 'syntax poems' for performance, when his work is still alive, still carrying out its own propulsive transformation?

From 2014 to 2016, during and after my Judith E. Wilson Poetry Fellowship at the University of Cambridge, I had access to a blackbox studio theatre, a dark space with insulated walls and movable seating. With a group of people including genius theatre maker Jeremy Hardingham and brilliantly inventive students Paige Smeaton and Hope Doherty, I started to evolve a way of immersing audiences in the feeling of the world of a poem, rather than staging standard readings of texts (microphone and lectern, audience forced to face one way and be worshipful). We were not interested, either, in a conventional dramatisation of a poetic script. Instead, immersive experiments became the context for events including reading of full texts alongside what I call 'syntax poems' gleaned from them. The syntax poems offer traces of a way of being *with and inside* Carter's poetry. They are not the kind of indepenent verbal artefacts called responses or reworkings. They are rearrangeable elements for future experiments. They require several voices, and best with bodies in motion.

One of our primary desires in creating these syntax poems was to free a feeling of movement to rise out of Carter's words. Carter's poetry is restless and has been recited in conditions of unrest. Being alone with a book prioritises its equally valuable, but less excitable, aspects. A solo reader might pause over the density of Carter's language. Its fishermen, protesters, flowers and streets are evocative, symbolic, yet specific. Place ingrained in feeling seems to encourage researched reading. Sparse details can be unfurled into Guyanese realities. We, on the contrary, appreciated without wanting to dwell.

How to attain the desired feeling of movement? In transreading Carter to produce syntax poems, we concentrated on features of the language where activity happens, such as verbs and prepositions. For example, the Creole verb form 'I come' can mean 'I came' or 'I come'; in a poem, an understanding of this doubleness may allow past and present to co-exist. Another example: Carter's incantatory, obsessive joining or piling up of elements by 'in' or 'of' can feel overwhelming, like a kind of tilting of the poetic ground. We wanted to induce that vertigo in the audience; we would not skip, like the eye can, over the *act* of joining in order to fetishise *what* is joined. Further, we also felt that Carter's 'I' is so often extensive, inclusive, that to embody his texts simultaneously in various overlapping readings and actions might produce more of a sense of the *I that can be we* than any amount of explanation could.

Together and alone, silently and aloud, we kept re-reading selected Carter texts, at first 'simply' for syntax and features which activate movement. We did not care to 'shred', 'collage' or 'fracture'. Fearfully and lovingly, with the energy of our watered, out-of-breath bodies and voices, we tried to uncover, create and assemble mobile skeletons and provocative patterns of words, with enough colourful shreds of 'meaning' for the audience to follow the dance.

Carter's long poem, 'I Am No Soldier', which ends with the famous summoning of an 'astronomer of freedom' and secular hymn to the glittering potentiality seeded in ourselves, passes from a recognisably Guyanese opposition of soldiers in a jungle to poets in jail cells, through now challenging sections (praise of Mao Tse Tung) and vast visions of resistance that call on named parts of the world, to the politically engaged *and* aesthetically driven artist's conclusion 'I am this poem like a sacrifice'. We decided to invite whatever Cambridge audience we could muster into the world of this work. We also decided to be true to our own backgrounds, bringing in individual ways of connecting with or departing from the text, in the belief that a vivid self-honesty might electrify the audience into their own revulsions or connexions.

It was important to re-present Carter's world/work in ways that would be recognisable to readers who have grown up with his words and are linked to his region, yet which those entirely unfamiliar with it would be free to enter.

As people filed into the blackbox, finding scant seating facing no particular way, they were distracted from the fact that a long fence of sharp wire hived off much of the right length of the room. To their left was a schoolroom, where tall Jeremy in the form of a colonial schoolmaster used his beautiful voice to berate and question two students, teaching them prescriptively about Martin Carter's poetry and the right way to interpret it. This was as close as the audience got to a 'straight' reading. The lesson was not entirely oppressive nonsense; we made sure to smuggle in useful background information about Carter, his poetics and his time. This was justifiable, also being part of the play.

Like any good colonial schoolmaster, Jeremy failed to notice that the students, Hope and Paige, were dressed as mimes. Their answers turned increasingly unruly and imaginative – true to another aspect of Carter, his naturally enigmatic and quasi-modernist intellectual approach to innovation, in direct line from fellow Guyanese poet A.J. Seymour, with whom T.S. Eliot had corresponded. Eventually the mimes broke down the classroom and escaped.

During this time, dressed in white, I wandered through the studio like an itinerant preacher from a Welsh tradition of which Paige had told me, and which sparked associations for me with rhapsodic and ecstatic spiritual traditions in the Caribbean. In the style of a Carter-crazed divine, I recited 'I Am No Soldier' from memory, in its entirety and in fragments, over and over again, as if trying to convert, inspire or intimidate my fellows. This character allowed me to sound the poem in its full sonority and musicality.

Moving from the schoolroom to the street – spaces of Carter's society – we quick-changed in the open centre of the blackbox. Suddenly appearing as would-be revolutionaries and persecuted ordinary folk, we were in the jail and the yard, inside and outside the barbed wire, making poem-placards.

We passed through other movement, vocal and costume sequences. We hoped to make the text inhabit areas of life and styles of being human and verbal that make sense in the world of 'I Am No Soldier', but which would be invisibilised in a lectern reading to the seated bodies of listeners. We paid homage to the polytheisms of the Caribbean, having a ceremony in which we passed out and came to life again ridden by Carter, whispering and chanting antiphonal syntax poems, our stripped-down word-patterning, so that they were less versions than manifestations, and the airy structure of his meanings began to rise and swing. Finally, we danced the dance of constellations, holding on to each other's long black and silver scarves, calling on the astronomer of freedom, rejoicing beyond all bounds and including anyone in the audience who wished to take part.

The audience effectively heard the whole text delivered in several different modes, as well as gaining an insight into symbolic and representative social environments *by being in them with us* and *having them co-exist in one blackbox*. They also heard a living, not anatomised, version of practical criticism and close reading – which is what the syntax poems also offer.

Although the syntax poems themselves are divided up on the page less like projective poetry than perhaps like medieval polyphony, ideally realised by at least two voices, it is crucial to remember that they do emerge from a linear reading of the source texts. When printed out, they look misleadingly like a sequence. Their intended effect arrives if words jump and jumble on the page in a way that informs the performance, and if the audience does not feel they have listened to 'readers of poetry', but rather participated in a sense of call and response, cry and chorus, intimate camaraderie. We hope this may be an invitation to others not only to read Carter, but to bring the life in poetry (not 'bring poetry to life'!) into immersive and visionary spaces.

Letter from Cadiz

James Womack

Half of the restaurant sticks out over the sea: a suspended dining-room with aluminium tables and paper tablecloths and driftwood floorboards flecked and grating with sand. The other diners sit outside on the beach itself, the legs of their chairs in the bright sullen water. Clumps of seaweed and mixed detritus shredding and shifting in the semi-dormant waves. You lean out and look into the weeds and catch the truth of that poem you quite like: Jorie Graham, the one where 'the minnows, thousands, swirl / themselves, each a minuscule muscle'.

It is dirty, a haphazard careless dirtiness that is not unpleasant, but is simply the result of living in a world of sand and salt, where freshness is a myth and humidity levels hang around eighty percent twelve months of the year. Your clothes feel damp even before you put them on; paperbacks decide to imitate the surrounding Atlantic and twist themselves into waves that after a few days slump saturated back into flatness.

You are here to eat. You eat aliens: deep-fried sea anemones that are sacs of salted jelly; clams that have swung open like Bibles. You tear off and suck the heads of *gambas rojas*, enjoying the salty brain. Your son throws breadsticks to the fish. You eat *cazón*, dogfish. The serving plates are passed round until they are empty. You eat chips and fried green peppers, and drink beer from frozen glasses.

Today you don't really talk to your wife's family, Óscar and his girlfriend, but when you do, you talk about nothing. This is not the place for political discussion – you are here to eat – but today in particular nothing seems to catch. Conversations start up and fail, and you cover this failure with chips and clams. It's odd, you are not uncomfortable, but there seems today to be a wall between you and the rest of the world. You feel happier looking at the sea, the little fish 'making of themselves a / visual current'.

Housman: 'the sea is a large department; [but] as a subject of poetry is somewhat barren'. But today you understand it, can see why children love the sea, how it works as a first introduction to the world of metaphor. All the straightforward questions and answers: the impermanence of humanity, the sandcastles being sucked away by the rising tide, this vast indifferent colourful object, the same material always rearranged in subtly different combinations. All so obvious and nonetheless true. What will the crabs leave after I drown, you think to yourself. The steel plate from your skull.

This morning, before coming out to the restaurant, you walked through the old town. Manuel lived here when he was younger, and knows how it works, but Herminia, who grew up five hundred metres away, on the avenue, claims always to get lost in its alleys. You yourself feel uncomfortable here: a world made out of backstreets, most of which you think you have never seen before, even as you walk them over again. It's a fractal city: the closer you look at it, the more detail it reveals. Not to mention the history, the layers upon layers. The oldest continually inhabited city in Europe: you are constantly surprised by Phoenician noses and eyes, Roman faces, Celtic faces, the faces of Al-Andalus. The centre of the garum industry at the time of Augustus: fish guts fermenting and dripping through tight-plaited baskets.

Byron wrote his worst poem here, in a fog of coital longing: 'born beneath a brighter sun / For love ordained the Spanish maid is, / And who, when fondly, fairly won, / Enchants you like the Girl of Cadiz?' Who indeed. Slightly better are his descriptions of the place in his letters, although they still give the impression of being written by a bigoted lovesick cartoon wolf, his eyes popping and his tongue unrolling over the table: 'Cadiz, sweet Cadiz! – it is the first spot in the creation. The beauty of its streets and mansions is only excelled by the loveliness of its inhabitants. For, with all national prejudice, I must confess the women of Cadiz are as far superior to the English women in beauty as the Spaniards are inferior to the English in every quality that dignifies the name of man.' Or this, from a letter to his mother: 'Long black hair, dark languishing eyes, *clear* olive complexions, and forms more graceful in motion than can be conceived by an Englishman used to the drowsy, listless air of his countrywomen, added to the most becoming dress, and, at the same time, the most decent in the world, render a Spanish beauty irresistible.'

Enough wooziness, enough décolletage. It's a city built out of reclaimed rock from the sea, fossils in every wall you touch. The city fights the sea; the sea fights back: Cádiz is a shifting space. When your older brother came to visit a year or so ago, you walked him past the port to the best ice-cream parlour in town. On the way home, he suddenly stopped, owlishly confused: 'Wasn't there a block of flats here when we came by earlier?' One of the regular seven-storey cruise liners had slipped away, changing the configuration of the labyrinth. But today, for an afternoon at least, you have broken out, and everything is much simpler. You were just here to eat.

When you have eaten, you all walk out of the back door of the restaurant onto a small weedy beach. Your son wants to run into the water; your brother-in-law holds him back and swings him round, both of them laughing and apparently happy. There are some dead dried crabs laid up on a pile of driftwood. 'I am free to go. / I cannot of course come back. Not to this. Never.' Herring gulls. Stray cats. A placard tells you that all stray cats here are captured and neutered before being allowed back into the wild. A blue European flag flies lazily above the restaurant. You are suddenly very tired, and feel very alone.

R. S. Thomas *redivivus*

DAVID WHITING

'Watching' by R.S. Thomas has been hiding in plain sight for over fifty-five years, a poem published only once (to the best of my knowledge), in a long forgotten 1962 anthology. Thomas never chose to collect it, and the poem was overlooked more recently when Tony Brown and Jason Walford Davies edited R.S. Thomas's 'Uncollected Poems' (Bloodaxe) in 2013, bringing together many pieces that had only previously appeared in various periodicals and limited editions. Tony Brown tells me it is the first poem to emerge since their book came out. Here is the text of the poem.

> One life was not long enough.
> Although the light fused many times
> In the course of his stay, the rare bird
> Never came, coasting the marsh,
> Where the rush burned. He lived knowing
> That eyes not his had seen it depart
> In a far summer. His thought compelled it
> In cold skies, where it hung back
> And waited for the snow to deploy
> Its white army. There was room on the bog,
> Where the man pondered; the still pools'
> Cameras were focused, but day after day
> They took nothing but the blank sky's
> Incident, or at night the stars,
> The spent flakes of remoter storms.

The anthology it appeared in was *The Wind and the Rain; An Easter Book for 1962*, edited by Neville Braybrooke (1923–2001). Braybrooke was a poet, novelist, editor and biographer. *The Wind and the Rain* began in 1940 as a Catholic-leaning literary magazine edited by Braybrooke and enterprising fellow pupils at Ampleforth College. In 1962 it was briefly revived as a yearbook of prose and poetry, published by Secker and Warburg. Contributors apart from Thomas included David Jones, Elizabeth Jennings, Ruth Pitter and Vernon Watkins. I owned a copy many years ago, parted with it, and only found another copy in 2018, realising that the Thomas poem it contained, written when he was vicar of Eglwysfach, had never been reprinted.

Tony Brown wrote to me:

The first thing that struck me about the poem, given the subject matter and the title, was the reference 'the rare bird', which of course occurs in 'Sea-watching', which was not published until 1975 (in Laboratories of the Spirit): 'Ah, but a rare bird is / rare. It is when one is not looking, / at times one is not there / that it comes'. That poem is of course an account of spiritual searching / longing; the bird is also God (though R.S. preferred to refer to some formulation like 'Ultimate Reality')... And the rare bird does come in the later poem, albeit when the speaker is not there. There is no such suggestion in the 1962 poem.

I'd want to say that 'Watching' is also not just about bird watching (R.S. was an avid bird watcher). Essentially it seems to me to be an expression of mood, not just about the elusive bird. The bird has associations of a better (happier?) time / state of being ('... eyes not his had seen it depart / In a far summer.'), a summer which is manifestly in contrast to the present of 'cold skies'. That 'blank sky' towards the end is again surely evocative of a mood of spiritual and imaginative dullness, a sort of ennui? I think I'd find this in the poem anyway, but the period R.S. spent at Eglwysfach includes some of his most unhappy years, as man and priest... this is, in my view, a poem about the speaker's emotional and spiritual state, in a landscape that gives him no response (that blank sky), a sense of alienation from what might be; that 'far summer'.

My gratitude to Professor Tony Brown, Caroline Moorey (Estate of R.S. Thomas) and Random House.

Remembering Bernard Loughlin

MARY O'MALLEY

The Tyrone Guthrie Centre at Annaghmakerrig is a retreat for artists very close to the Cavan-Monaghan border. It is situated in drumlin country – if you shout, you can hear the echo rolling away eerily into the distance. It is not far from the border with Northern Ireland and it is landlocked.

Bernard Loughlin and his wife Mary were its first directors and played host to writers, musicians, painters and composers from 1981, when it formally opened, to 1999 when he and Mary left.

They built it into a home from home for an ever changing population of artists where friendships were formed and work was made and fun was had; but what I remember mostly are quiet days spent working in rooms far grander than anything most of us had at home, a lively dinner every evening, and quiet, often solitary walks.

I went there as a young mother in about 1990, after my first book was published.

I wrote a brief description of what I wanted to work on and got accepted. Then I panicked. I had almost no money but I knew I must pay 'what I could afford'. This led to anxiety and to me paying slightly more than I could afford.

Another cause of anxiety that first visit was the Director himself. I had seen him on TV and he terrified me. He spoke in paragraphs, was better read than most people and didn't suffer fools.

When I rang up to ask how I'd get to the house from the nearest bus stop several miles away, the response was terse. There was a taxi or I could hitch. This was Border Country in times of trouble. All I knew of Monaghan was in the poetry of Patrick Kavanagh. When the bus got to Clones, it was almost dark. I hitched and accepted a lift from a man with a child, thinking this would be a safe bet. The child immediately hopped out and said: 'Daddy, I don't want to go in the boot, don't make me.' Luckily, he didn't.

After an interminable and slightly weird drive, we reached the sign for the centre. Someone had shot at it, probably for fun. The farmer wanted to get a look inside the house so that he could report the 'goings on' which, he assured me with a leer, were well known. I fled.

Bernard showed my room, pointed out the fridge and the kettle in the kichen and I was alone in Monaghan.

Dinner, always obligatory, helped. There were painters, who were welcoming, and a renowned concert pianist I had only seen on TV. He was very kind to us newcomers and gave everyone lifts into Newbliss. The music room was next door to mine and I used to leave the door open a chink the better to hear him practice. One of the painters said I could look in on his studio if I wanted when he wasn't working. Slowly I settled in.

At the end of the eight-day visit, during which I slept uneasily every night, I had the bones of my second book, the long sequence I had come to write practically finished.

For the next eight years, I came back regularly.

Bernard ran things in a way that facilitated the intense concentration needed at certain stages in a writer's work. He had rules, and the rules were there to be kept. If you started upstairs with a mug of tea he would appear out of nowhere with a saucer. There was a touch of the old-style reverend mother to Bernard. No television was another rule, easy to keep since there was none, and he didn't like sick people. There was no politics allowed at dinner. Annaghmakerrig was, I think, one of the first genuine cross-border initiatives and well ahead of its time, with people coming from both sides of the border.

Bernard had unerring sense of what artists needed, and he made sure we got it in spades: time to work in a house that was also a home. Mary saw to that. She also saw that we ate well; she and Doreen were two of the best cooks in Ireland and the fridge was always well stocked for lunch and snacks. I once heard a visiting journalist remark to Bernard that, 'You do yourselves well here.' Bernard fixed him with the gimlet eye and said, 'I don't subscribe to the starving-artist-in-the-garret philosophy here.' It was the Loughlin's creed that while under their stewardship, artists lived well.

His monument, as well as his own books, is the art of a generation, the books, the music, sculpture and theatre he so generously enabled for so long. He had an office, and he was an administrator, the very best. I was never asked to fill out a form.

He designed the garden at Annaghmakerrig, making much of it himself. When he wasn't in the office, he was outside working with a spade and hoe.

News of Bernard's death in an accident in Farrera, Catalonia, where he has lived since leaving Annaghmakerrig, has brought great sadness and regret. He died in an accident while working, in his garden, in the high Pyrennees.

Ar dheis De go raibh a anam.

On Being Translated

IAN SEED

Although I was expecting it, I could hardly believe my eyes when a copy of *Sognatore di sogni vuoti* (Edizioni Ensemble) arrived through my letterbox.

A little over two years ago, Iris Hajdari, whom I had met a few months before with her partner the Italian-Albanian poet Gëzim Hajdari, wrote to me saying that she would like to translate my collection *Makers of Empty Dreams* (Shearsman, 2014) into Italian. Apart from a handful of poems translated into Dutch for a web magazine (now nowhere to be found), no one had ever translated my writing before. I felt especially honoured because as a younger man I spent a number of years working in Italy as a teacher and translator. Many of the prose poems in *Makers* are set in northern Italian cities, towns and hills. At the same time, I didn't quite believe the translation was actually going to happen. This may have something to do with the fact that, apart from a few bad poems in my youth, I have come to writing relatively late in life. Almost any publication can seem a bit too good to be true. Besides, I knew that Iris worked full-time and was expecting a baby. Life gets in the way of the best-laid plans. I replied to say how delighted I was, but also that there was no rush. I heard nothing until out of the blue eighteen months or so later, I received a draft copy to check the Italian translation of *Makers of Empty Dreams*.

As I read through, I had the strange sensation of being spied upon naked or while up to something not quite decent. Odd and illogical to feel that way since the book in its English form was already out there, had been reviewed, and so presumably read. What was it then about a translation? I can only answer by saying that as a result of my own experience as a translator, I also come to feel that I know the authors of the originals in a way that no one else does. I am making a series of judgements on them – or at least on their creative work – each time I make a choice of which word or phrase I use in my English version. Now this was being done to me.

I went through the Italian text carefully. I thought it beautifully captured the spirit of the original, but I also made a list of suggestions for changes. We discussed these in a long video conference call. Gëzim was by Iris's side, holding and entertaining their baby daughter while making several recommendations of his own. At the end of the call, I made it clear that the final version in Italian was up to Iris. But I had mixed feelings about doing this. A part of me wanted to keep control, even though I knew this was impossible – it was not me this time who was the translator. The Italian text of *Makers of Empty Dreams* was not my creation...

Yet now that it is has become finally and truly real to me through its physical presence, I find myself worrying once more about the relationship of the translated version to the original. For example, the title in Italian, *Sognatore di sogni vuoti*, translated literally back into English would be 'Dreamer of Empty Dreams'. This implies more of a lyrical 'I' than the original, and perhaps hints at more autobiography than fiction. Yet there is truth in the spirit of this translation: different narrative voices compete in *Makers*, but there is also a sense of them belonging to one person. The pieces in *Makers* are not autobiographical in any factual sense; however, through their small fictions they try to shape autobiographical experience.

At a more technical level, differences between languages can create problems. For example, the title of one of the poems 'Town Centre' (first published in *PNR* 214) is translated as 'Centro Città'. I suppose 'town centre' *could* also mean 'city centre' (though it is not quite the same thing), and another possible choice in Italian, 'Centro Cittadina' (literally small city), while more accurate, just does not have the same ring to it. Yet still I fret as Prufrock did, that it 'is not what I meant at all, / That is not what I meant at all'. But then the act of writing is itself a form of translation, and of course language is forever slippery. I realise that just as I have learnt to let my own poems make their own way in the world like little feral animals, so I must let their Italian cousins do the same.

'While the tree lived, he in these fields lived on'

JOHN CLEGG

Now Carcanet's Fyfield*Books* imprint has yielded to Carcanet Classics, it may be worth clearing up some confusion in the two sentences and a quotation which were printed opposite the title page for the duration of the series. 'Fyfield*Books* take their name from the Fyfield elm in Matthew Arnold's 'Scholar Gypsy' and 'Thrysis'. The tree stood not far from the village where the series was originally devised in 1971.' This was followed by these lines from 'Thrysis':

> Roam on! The light we sought is shining still.
> Dost thou ask proof? Our tree yet crowns the hill,
> Our scholar travels yet the loved hill-side.

The problem is that the tree with Arnoldian associations near South Hinksey (the village where the series was devised) isn't the Fyfield Elm at all; the small village of Fyfield is a good ten miles away. The Fyfield Elm, also known as the Tubney Tree, was a hollow wych-elm about thirty inches in diameter marking the parish boundary (at an important crossroads) between Fyfield and Tubney. It doesn't crown any hill; it nestles in a dip, or rather nestled, since when I went looking for it, any trace was long gone. (The last record I can find, thoroughly rotten by this point and its name long forgotten, is from 1986.) When Arnold says 'I know the Fyfield tree', it isn't a recapitulation of 'our tree-topped hill' but his thoughts drifting through the other landmarks and timemarks he shared with Arthur Hugh Clough: 'I know the wood which hides the daffodil, / I know the Fyfield tree, / I know what white, what purple fritillaries / The grassy harvest of the river fields, / Above by Ensham, down by Sanford, yields...'

So where is 'our tree' in the lines from 'Thrysis'? It is almost certainly in the field called 'Matthew Arnold's Field' or 'Signal Elm Field', bought from Chilswell Farm (Arnold's 'Childsworth Farm') by All Souls' College in 2009. It is also almost certainly, despite what Arnold says, not an elm. Arnold personally identified the tree to A.C. Bradley: it was an oak, known locally as 'the umbrella tree' because of its odd crown (the central tree in the photo, taken by Henry Taunt in 1925). It is still thriving – a misidentification on a popular walking website has led to it being frequently confused with a large broken oak nearby (possibly the tree to the right in Taunt's photo?), so many of the pictures on the internet represent it as being dead. The Oxford Preservation Trust's website has an image of the correct tree. The intermittent collapse and regrowth of the tree's crown across the twentieth century has been strangely coincident with the rise and fall of Clough's poetic reputation.

from The Notebooks of Arcangelo Riffis

M A R I U S   K O C I E J O W S K I

'Are there any fish in Afghanistan?' I asked my Afghan fishmonger once. 'No,' he replied, 'it's why I'm here.' I think he got one over me because when I got home I checked to see if there are fish in Afghanistan and I discovered there are at least one hundred and thirty species. Now I'll have to ask him whether they are, at least some of them, edible. The walk of approximately two miles to the North End Road market where I buy my fish and vegetables takes me through Margravine Cemetery which is pleasingly dilapidated and would make an ideal setting for a 1930s horror film. The gravestones are at precarious angles, many of them, and in places the ground about them swells as if the dead are pushing up from underneath, furious that we've forgotten them. *Add prayers and proper words to the fixed fires.* This morning, as usual, I walked down the main avenue of the cemetery and then I exited at the gate that goes into Field Road, which then turns left into Greyhound Road, and it was there, where the two roads meet, that I saw a young woman in a summery pink dress pause, raise one leg, and, perfectly balancing herself on the other one, remove her shoe and shake out of it a small pebble. I marvelled at the sheer grace with which an ordinary enough procedure had become a balletic one. There was in this eroticism of a kind that's almost too subtle for language. She had beautiful legs, which, I suppose, helped set in motion the mind's processes. As I turned away from her, she now back on terra firma, I looked up and saw a man strapped to the top of the steeple of Saint Andrew's Church which is further on down Greyhound Road. I could hear the tap-tap-tapping of a hammer which I could not see at that distance. As I got closer, I could see a large yellow plastic bucket beside him. This intrigued me. When I got to the entrance of the church I discovered his workmate standing below, looking up at him, and probably awaiting instructions. As I was now comparatively close, the sight of the man directly above me was sufficient to induce in me feelings of vertigo. I asked the man on the ground what the man on the steeple was doing. 'You see up there where the finial is? He's tacking new stone where the old's become unstable.' 'So that's why you're wearing a hard hat,' I jested, 'in order to protect yourself from heaven's wrath.' Poor joke. He pointed to a small pile of stones. It was then I understood the purpose of the yellow bucket. By means of rope and pulley it was used to lower the decrepit stone.

Maybe I'm overly impressionable, so be it, but with the young woman removing the pebble from her shoe and the man so precariously tethered to the steeple and with the two of them, one on terra firma and the other in the skies, inhabiting the same moment, suddenly I was overwhelmed with a wondrous sense of delicacy and balance. It took me a while, though, to make the connection. As I've said elsewhere, the air is the full of connections waiting to be made, but only if we have eyes behind our eyes. There'd be no poetry otherwise. Balance or what Arcangelo calls 'a middle ground' is what a writer most requires. There can be no striving for it because it will not be forced into being and it is what my friend 'too wrought up & agitated for creativity' most sorely wanted for in life. Did he ever achieve that balance? I think not. As a small boy it was, he told me, something of which he was continually, one might even say *intentionally*, deprived.

February 1, 1978. Cool. A child beholds his wonders & comforts in a fourth dimension, unique to childhood, which cannot be initiated or contrived in later life, only vaguely remembered & deferred to. Any attempt, deliberate or otherwise, at the former can be disastrous indeed – except within the natural & mysterious workings of artistic inspiration. Spots or, rather, relics in this garden – say, a book, a film, a place or a piece of music – can be revisited & viewed or considered in the second dimension of adulthood, and the result can often be a heart-unsettling experience: the essential magic, the green-foliage poetry & music, is forever gone from this life. But if one is careful, and approaches these relics with deference & a certain reverence, one can recover nuances & impressions of the magic with which these things were once invested.

Summertime: how old was I, six? An outdoor visit with neighbours in our backyard. I remember as solid fact that I was doing no harm, no mischief. The neighbours were chatting merrily. To my own utter astonishment, as well as everyone else's, my father suddenly caught me up, thrashed me brutally in a degrading manner. I made no sound, uttered no cries – after his sport I was dropped on the lawn – stunned, shamed – my head swimming.

'Get him inside,' he rasped to his wife.

The next morning I said hello to little Sandy Jo next door, who could barely look at me for the shameful scene of which I was the object just the night before, the neighbours too caught up in their own conversation to notice I'd done nothing wrong. I doubt if I got much, if any, sympathy from them. My father did it solely to score points with them, to show them what a tough dad he was, in the Milehi'-approved fashion. In their own twisted way, he & his wife seemed to be grooming me to be the *bad kid* of the family & neighbourhood – for the sheer unspeakable fun of the shaming & beatings. Crazy as it sounds, this is the only explanation I can find that clarifies so many of these memories that, where hitherto I could keep them at bay, are forcing themselves on me in these days & nights.

So many of the most beautiful memories of my childhood were followed by acts of indecent brutality at the hand of my father & the direct cause of one of them was a magical conversation I had with the hitherto aloof & haughty little blond girl near Mrs Austin's backyard about God & other matters – this cost me the degradation of a skin thrashing of the kind which, far worse than physical pain, left me in a snarl of self-hatred & self-contempt. There was no real reason – there didn't have to be. No one had been frantically searching for me – a single call from our backyard & I'd have heard. My ugliest recollection involves my father's wife's delight in telling school chums & neighbourhood children of the degrading way her husband used to beat me. She would speak with genuine relish – this must have really 'turned her on', in '60s parlance – and it would fill me with the deepest mortification & humiliation. Indeed, I regarded this tattle of hers as more to be dreaded than the actual beatings. It affected some of the children in peculiar ways – they would seem to feel much of the same shame I felt, and avoided looking me in the eye.

Written at the head of the notebook that contains the above passage is a quotation from Thurman Wilkins's *Cherokee Tragedy – The Ridge Family and the Decimation of a People* (1970): 'The Cherokee fathers... seldom chided [their children] and never punished them with blows. For Cherokee parents believed that physical punishment of children only debased their minds and blunted their sense of honour.'

Letter from Wales

SAM ADAMS

A few months ago I received through the post a remarkable photograph, which I believe has not been widely published, as it certainly deserves to be. It is a fine black and white print of three iconic figures in the cultural life of Wales, R.S. Thomas, Kyffin Williams and Emyr Humphreys, and was taken at least eighteen years ago, for R.S. died in September 2000. The photographer was fortunate, or had planned with exceptional care, to get them together, etched with great clarity against a pale, plain background. All three are formally attired and peer seriously, or questioningly, at the lens; the occasion might have required a sober response to the photographer's request. R.S. came originally from Cardiff, but in later years settled in north Wales, the other two were born there. Their conversation would have been in Welsh. They belong to an earlier generation, one which witnessed in their own lifetimes enormous changes in the working life, customs and beliefs of the people of Wales. R.S. was born in 1913; Kyffin Williams, who died in 2006, in 1918. Emyr Humphreys, born 1919, will be one hundred years old in April next year. All three dedicated their creative lives to Wales. Roland Mathias – who died in 2007, just short of his ninety-second birthday, lived through the same often devastating transformations and was equally imbued with devotion to the same cause – would have been a wonderful addition to the group.

Emyr Humphreys by M. Wynn Thomas, a new addition to the 'Writers of Wales' series, has just been published by the University of Wales Press to celebrate the writer's centenary. The series was originally intended to provide no more than an introduction to the selected writers and the vast majority are rather brief and do not have the apparatus of notes and index that characterises scholarly productions. In recent years the editorial approach to the series has changed in this respect, and entirely for the better. Wynn Thomas's latest addition to it provides, succinctly, a fuller, more perceptive account of the writer's life than any previously available, and as thorough and detailed a survey and analysis of Humphreys's prose and poetry as one could hope to see. He describes his subject as the 'last great survivor of the heroic age of twentieth century Welsh culture [...] [that] cohort of writers who dedicated their conspicuous talents to infusing political as well as cultural energy into Welsh life sufficient to arouse their country out of the long torpor of its meekly subservient position within a profoundly anglo-centric "British" polity.' The book is distinguished by the sinew and strength of Wynn Thomas's writing and his unerring selection of example and witness illustrating the nature and scale of this rearguard action to preserve some vestige of the individuality represented by 'Wales' and 'Welsh'.

Emyr Humphreys comes from Trelawnyd, a village in the far north-eastern corner of Wales, close to the border with England, where his father was headmaster of the local C of E elementary school. The nearest towns, several miles away, are the anglicised coastal resorts of Rhyl and Prestatyn. His 'spirited and independent' mother, who came from a farming background, is identified by Thomas as the model of the resolute and mettlesome women that are prominent in his novels and have contributed substantially to his deserved reputation as a creator of female characters. His 'quiet and mild' father, originally from Ffestiniog, of Welsh-speaking, slatequarrying stock, suffered for the rest of his life from the effects of gassing in the First World War. A Nonconformist by up-bringing, he had converted to the Anglican Church and was withal contentedly anglicised. That, in his youth, the novelist flirted briefly with the notion of becoming an Anglican cleric is perhaps a salute to paternal influence. Certainly, in his case, it signals a serious commitment to Christian belief. When he married, he joined his wife among the *Annibynwyr*, the Welsh Congregationalists.

As a sixth former at Rhyl County School, already sympathetic to the Nationalist cause, he began to learn Welsh, which as his command of the language increased, 'enabled him to read a geographical and cultural landscape that had previously been illegible'. By his late teens he was attending Plaid Cymru meetings, at one of which he met Saunders Lewis, whom he admired both as writer and as one of the trio imprisoned for setting fire to the hutments of the bombing school at Penyberth on Llŷn. Lewis remained a touchstone for the art and attitude of the developing writer.

In 1937 he entered UCW Aberystwyth, where his studies were interrupted by the war. Like Roland Mathias and notable others, he became a conscientious objector on religious grounds. He accepted direction to work on the land and then, in 1943, following training, served with Save the Children Fund in Egypt and, in the wake of the Allied advance, through Italy. The end of the war found him helping to run a large refugee camp in Florence, where he became fluent in Italian, and a confirmed Italophile and Welsh European. Thomas shows that Humphreys's Nationalism never implied turning inwards. Rather it was a creative commitment to Wales in a European context. He believed, in his own words, 'to be more European, we need first to be more Welsh'.

Returned from Italy, he married and, after teacher training at Bangor, joined the staff of a technical college in Wimbledon. In London he formed important friendships with, among others, Anthony Powell, Huw Weldon, Patrick Heron and Graham Greene, then editor of *The Spectator*, whose advice and encouragement were important factors in his continuing development. His teaching career continued at a grammar school in Pwllheli, but having won the Somerset Maugham Award with his fourth novel, *Hear and Forgive*, in 1955 he left education to join BBC Wales as a producer of radio, and later TV, drama. In this capacity, it was entirely consistent with his European outlook that he put on plays by Dürrenmatt and Brecht and commissioned a Welsh translation of *Waiting for Godot* from Saunders Lewis. His experience in the role also drew him into contact with many of the most significant personalities in the cultural life of Wales at that time, and contributed to an evolution in the style and narrative structure of subsequent novels. In 1965, he left the BBC to establish a drama department at UCNW Bangor. There he exploited his knowledge of the media to the benefit of his students, but finding he was less productive personally, he resigned in 1971 to devote his energies to writing.

Humphreys's first novel, *The Little Kingdom*, though published in 1946, was written while he was in Egypt. His output in fiction has since extended to a further twenty-one novels (including a seven volume novel sequence 'Land of the Living') and four collections of short stories. There have been, besides, an important book on Welsh cultural history, *The Taliesin Tradition* (1983), and numerous essays and shorter pieces. He began as a poet and has continued to produce poetry as it were in the margins of his long life as a writer: *Ancestor Worship* (1970) and *Collected Poems* (1999) will be followed later this year by another big collection, *Shards of Light*.

His home ground, Wales, is the permanent setting for his creative expression, but his theme is humanity and its implications are universal. All his writing is strikingly characterised by intellectual and moral consistency. If I were to pluck a single example, *Outside the House of Baal* (1965) is unquestionably a novel of European significance.

Below: R. S. Thomas, Kyffin Williams and Emyr Humphreys, Pentrefelin, 1999. (© Matthew Thomas)

'Small precise things'

From the Journals, 8 March 2008

R. F. LANGLEY

Overcast, altostratus, almost raining most of the day and a wind getting up which will reach 80mph, the papers say, in the West and South tomorrow night. Not so fierce here, but blowy. Edward's Lane, after picking up a bottle of milk from Clarke's in Low Road, this morning. Celandine opening quite thickly now on that north bank, which is of course south facing. Amongst it I notice a small white flower and pluck a piece of it to check it, and one leaf of it looks so much like the leaf of English scurvy grass in the book that I jump to this identification, and begin to juggle with the possibility that it is a hybrid with common scurvy grass, or even Danish, or early scurvy grass since that flowers now rather than in April, and has spread because of railway ballast, and the railway bridge is close by.

But I go back this afternoon, with B out prompting at Louise's play at the Cut, and take a proper sample, finding that the plant has seedpods, thin, upright and dark, protruding among the flower heads, and upper leaves much thinner than the one I was looking at this morning, and even that the rounder lower leaves do not slope into their stems so much. It is hairy bittercress, as might be expected from the date and the position on a field bank rather than on mudflats or riverside.

Looking more carefully at the bank this time, I find that the red deadnettle is out in some profusion, packed beds of it, and chickweed is flowering, and speedwell, as well as the the celandine and primroses and periwinkle. The 'blackthorn' by the church must be cherry... the bark has horizontal lines of glands across it, and there are not enough real thorns, only some accidental thin stubs that confuse me. The white flowers are not in umbels, though; they are running along the twigs. Small precise things exercise me again. To go a second walk to check a flower amuses me. I meet Charles[1] coming from the shop, and we talk of the coming winds.

I think of the two figures in the far left background of Poussin's *Landscape with a man being killed by a snake*, and how they dominate the picture by being so minute, so that their presumably casual conversation as they meet on the road oddly dominates the drama and death and horror in the foreground, seeming more powerful, more extensive, deeper in, further off, requiring hard peering to discover it and begin to interpret it, and thus catching up the viewer in the problems of visibility and knowing what is there, so that the landscape and the figures seem more equal, the human subsumed in the scenery, the dip in the bank through which one sees them, the tree that overarches them though it is a long way this side of them, the wall with the tiny ruined window showing sky through it, which is further back and closer to the edge even than they are. Interest, concern and attention requiring effort are caught into a pure focus by such smallness, happen, as it were, in recession, so that one has to go after them, instead of pressing forward at you to make a major point. They feel more a part of continuity than the foreground death, more true to the continuous that needs to be registered and coped with.

Hairy bittercress, which is scarcely at all hairy. A misnomer. And along the greasy polish of the lax stem of chickweed there is one line of hairs. How odd! What for? How come? And human beings as part of the scene, not its focus.

As Charles and I stand to talk by her house, the torso of Kirsten Bartholomew appears above us, over the hedge, and she greets us, her hair, her face, voice, above us and to the side and not central as looked for, reminding me... reminding me... of the two people[2]... women... in the arbour down lower than the road, seated, one looking at the Bellman as he walks past on his way down into the village, the deep road ahead between houses, running under a bridge, turning left, a lighted window on the curve so facing up to us, the Bellman glancing down at the woman... in the etching though not in the painting... and swinging his bell, the roofs at angles running away, the church tower on the far side of the village, the mountains beyond that, the darkness... human beings in subordinate positions, making little interventions, not obtruding or taking a central position, being a part of what is happening rather than taking a hold on it, companionship with each other and the scene, Kirsten over the hedge, red deadnettle on the bank.

edited by Barbara Langley

NOTES
[1] Charles Mullett, a Bramfield neighbour.
[2] *The Bellman* by Samuel Palmer, etching and painting in the 2005 British Museum exhibition.

'Llandeilo Churchyard' and other poems

G.C. WALDREP

Llandeilo Churchyard (1)

When I went to visit the holy well I found a little child there. He was texting on his
        phone. He didn't look up.
Water lifting water, read the plaque by the estate pump-house.
So much of my life has been spent in postures of waiting. (What literature & faith
        hold in common.)
Radiant expectation, the yew's gathered cloths, the elm's crippled genuflection.
We are all invited to the Festival of the Senses. Some blindfolded, others as vendors
        of blindfolds.
Both waking & sleeping I study lichens. I know more about them in my dreams than in
        waking life.
The mowers again, this time in their Welsh masks, their festival masks. I doff my hat &
        step aside.
Blue light of the iPhone in the holy well's dank recess. I make nothing up, I assure you.
I kept walking down that ancient street. Somewhere nearby, a local band covering CCR
        (badly, but with conviction).
Thirst says, You could have a drink, if you wanted to.
Devotional space, water's volume function. Open the book, close it, open it again.
Is the book about pain, you ask. That's a good question, I reply. (All questions are good,
        you insist.)
The ford, the ram, alluvial drift. Oxbows of the flood plain, faith's water cycle.
I watched from the terrace as the older man unloaded his cases of soda, his bottled
        juices.
You could buy gold here, or silver. Musical instruments handcrafted with artisanal care.
        Fabulous garments (the end of the world, etc.).
The police presence glistening like a droplet on skin. I don't necessarily mean human
        skin.
Drink this. It's on the dead, on the house (of the dead).
I recall being able to hit a high C with a purity of tone that made others jealous (& this
        frightened me, a little).
In those masses loosely classified as 'parodies', pressing the secular for its spangled
        plasma.
The yew as centrifuge, hurling everything it is & isn't toward its periphery. Don't think
        they're blind, the old woman warned me.
A celebrity promises to swim the Great Pacific Garbage Patch. 'Mind over matter', he
        intones.
I've made only two vows in my life. I broke one.
Heal the scalpel, heal the center's variant refrain.
At the Festival of the Senses, booths for eating, listening, touching. I lead the blind with
        a long, knotted rope.
Or, sometimes, music's faint meniscus, resting on something else: a voice, a stone, these
        Bartlett pears.
The boy did not look up at me, or into the water. What was he there for, then. Streaks of
        old coal at the cornice.
Maybe the book is about pain – since it flows through my hands. (This is in my dream.
        Because while I do look, I don't actually touch the water, don't let it touch me.)
Beside the basin, a damaged photograph, some wilted blossoms, something the field
        coughed up: asters, forget-me-nots.
A child's idea (gazing into his phone, his pale face lit with the blue light).
When I say the word 'filter' to myself, over & over again, it begins to sound like an organ
        of the body, something bruisable. Excisable.
The variant refrain, the luminous white cloth.
If you were an image would you wash or be washed. Would you have that choice.
I tip the wineglass over. Fortunately, it's empty.

I believe in neither ghosts nor mirrors, but am visited by both. They leave a
    pale residue as evidence of their passage.
The little train clanking past, Ffairfach, Llandybie, Ammanford. Swansea,
    eventually.
Aesthesia, affliction. To touch the *gods*, I thought I read.
Perhaps that is what the boy was doing, or thought he was doing, in the
    presence of water.
We will attend the pantomime another evening. From a distance, the sound of
    some mammal, crying.

Dryslwyn

The sheep are built of glass, metal, stone. They move so slowly. They do not, in
    any conventional way, burn.
The end of the world as a gothic arch, with nothing on the other side. Absolute
    nothing, zero-dimensional.
This is a false statement of the problem, because it lies about the nature of God.
    And yet we see ourselves compressed, reflected, in that point.
Cue the sheep's midnight pyre. They have witnessed nations. Their eyes tutor the
    hawthorn, the elderflower.
Rustle of my bootsteps among the winding grasses, their jubilant treasuries of
    sugar, light & earth. They neither lift nor are they veil. Nettle, campion.
But what are angels' tongues made of, I heard the child ask its mother, in the
    dingy shop. (They are made either of bread or of glass, or of the end of
    the world.)
Flatbed after flatbed of molded concrete bridge abutments heading south, that
    is, away from this place. A kestrel rides the thermals.
Feast of twine, feast of immaculate forgetting.
The earth is a prodigy & I am its house, I tell the children, arrayed around me in
    my dream. On their haunches, damp with drizzle.
We wake into math, sometimes gently, more often abruptly. We think math is a
    cruel master, but this, too, is error.
I make a list of what has gone missing from this place, & then I cross it out. Sing,
    my bruised rib commands.
Damage's sole memory, often constructed, is of not-damage. From these two
    poles, the triangulation of experience.
Bone, I hiss at the sheep. They thrash & quiver. Their eyes roll, slowly, on their
    slender eyestalks. They hum, low & in unison.
Perhaps these are not sheep. (But, the end of the world – etc.)
No one is interested anymore in the poem as a scrim, as something light passes
    through, by design. I press my pen against my thigh.
Let's clothe the narrow places with silk, while we have time, while we have silk.
    Parliament of the notochord, dismissed.
I go on touching the elder, the ash, the sycamore with my weak-twinned gaze.
    Let's think about thirst together.
That math allows for both bread & flight is simply astonishing. (The hazel, the
    beech, the cedar, the oak. The ash again.)
I lay my head on the hill's steep slope. *Depend* in the punitive sense.
The tall man said, at some point you cease to be beautiful, you are merely a freak.
    Can this be said of landscape. (The stone lambs, the glass lambs.)
I measure the math with my calipers, I trim it faithfully with my small sharp
    knife, I pare it back.
What we don't know is where, if anywhere, they buried their dead. (Beneath their
    living, I would expect you to offer, drily.)
Would you call what you do *wandering*, the gardener asked.
Ruin is tenable, it's not just a recitation of forms. I grasp it, wrote Averroes. We
    are deep into the default of love & love's parenthesis.
Grey, green, & blue, the emblems run. (The sheep recognize this, pull tightly to
    the centre of their demesne.)
Pity's rapid posture, at the mouth of the great net. The lambs with their heads
    full of eyes, studded with eyes, streaked & tacky pearls.
It means the same thing, my teacher told me, after the accident. Not ungently.

Carn Goch

Friend oxygen, I strip your creche, now it lies despoiled in the long light, the
  northern light.
This is the finest place, from which to watch the lives of others.
I am trying to understand something very, very large & yet enclosed, bounded. (That
  is, not God.)
In the red city I worked as an agent for a manufacturer of hooks. Models hung from
  my leather vest; I jangled when I walked.
Math feels very personal here, & physics, contact sports into which we're drafted.
One almost feels one could eat stones.
Invisible beings play their part in economies of value, that production process. (See:
  the Water Cycle, disarrangement of.)
I sit with my back to the ancient town, the saint's hermitage, the Kuznan takeaway.
Remember boldly the unexplained phenomena, the Fortean husks.
You would not be surprised by anything here, by design. Sleeplessness, the same
  sort of exposed promontory with its sheaves & musks.
White noise of a distant jet, wind, some saints' pulses emigrating, etc.
You are a brilliant star running parallel to mercy's page.
Now everything is available but nothing is known. The lichens I sit on may be
  hundreds of years old.
I wore my lightest, brightest shirt to the birthday celebration. I can't believe in
  mirrors here, can't even imagine.
Where the dead store their water is another question.
Athwart language the eye falters, turns inward, recites again the same menu
  choices.
She said, This place has not known Christ. – Now it has.
But if the saints had passed through it, in their long queues, their ragged robes. One
  end to the other, little flames.
For flame is the glory of bone, just as bone is the glory of breath.
To feel simultaneously *suspended* & *upheld*.
I have no one to share this place with but you, friend oxygen, friend thief.
Drink, then, last captain of the reconnaissance. Dedicate every guest, to the
  extension of guests.
There are no clocks here. I, a clockmaker, am both free & stung.
The Desert Mothers would have understood, would have gotten this exactly right,
  the silence. (The Desert Fathers would have robbed the stones to build their
  cells.)
In the end everything is rendered magnificently intangible. This is the logic of the
  Mass.
Here I feel only the lack of my love for God, whom I love. Here in the melisma of
  absolutes.
Make haste, friend, to solve the equation of iron. (And its brutal kings? Yes, its
  brutal kings.)
You will pass through a slow wreath of psalm-light.
You may go anywhere you want, where other animals have gone. (See, their brailled
  traces, their broken, discarded bells.)
The cathedral was entirely empty except for me, I mean my body.
I moved carefully, at the edge of God's stealth.
The great forms condescend to us. They bring new smells with them, the smell of
  fresh snow, for example, or the bright patois of mint.
I walked in that place with the war overhead, a caul. I felt at perfect peace, then
  recalled, for a moment, the Armenian genocide. All those empty masks.
Water lifting water, blood lifting blood.
The stone anthem, that I learned in my dream – & woke, later, humming.
Is not the hair of graves, partisan: you are mistaken. (I never want to bring a student
  here, to stoop to explanation.)
You could bleed here, if you wanted to, you could shed your blood. Would that
  change anything?
These are the generations of stones, the stones in their generations. (What must
  this hillside be like when nothing cries out.)
Abrade them softly, with the hands, as one would a lump of clay, or dough.
The cathedral of ribs, so bright & empty now. I mean, of our motives.

That was one of the most beautiful films I have ever seen, she told me. (We were in
     the nearly closed restaurant, after.)
I will invent some new language for this, I thought.
Look, the post van remembers its primitive dance. Likewise the flashing train.
Some things are difficult to understand: Ireland, Zoroastrianism, geophagy, plasma
     physics. But in fact they can be understood, as well as participated in.
I was so happy in my breathing there. I did not need to keep waking belief up, from
     its drugged sleep.
(When I was dying, it was my mother's job, every few hours, or several times an
     hour, to wake me. She shook me slightly, insistently, by the shoulder or the
     arm. She called my name.) (And I said, later, yes, belief is like that.)

Ode to GCHQ Bude

Oh GCHQ Bude, I love you.
You are like
a bunch of herons
getting sunburnt on a cliff.
You are like ostriches
reading encyclopedias
in the rain.
When it's not raining
you are like the discarded
clothing worn
by some giants
who are safely dead now.
Oh GCHQ Bude
tell me how the giants died.
That is what I want
to know, and you
are in the sordid business
of knowing.

I promise I will keep
looking the other
way as I saunter by, i.e.
that I will watch
the sea. Oh GCHQ Bude,
the sea loves you
even more than I do,
the sea massages your
extensive cable network.
It's not always easy
to see where the sea stops
and the air,
what we call air,
starts. Perhaps that's
what the giants were arguing
about, when they died.
Tell me, GCHQ
Bude, where I have left

my intention
to build a wall between
you and my date of birth.
Tell me what bargain
you have struck
with the felons of Finland.
Oh GCHQ Bude,
I am walking past you now
because I can,
and you are so very fine.
They say you have wings,
as angels do.
They say people
work inside your body,
little plasmas
stroking upstream
towards your giant's heart.

Llandyfeisant Church (1)

Consider myself a rival, consider myself arrived. Small life
knows this place, its nooks & swells. Trouble the grasses, trouble the stone.
Men placed stones here: this much is certain. Sun knows it, moon
knows it, palefly, angleworm. Christ knows & is known.
The Christ of stone, of the lizard's broad back. Inhume vs. subsume.
No space is 'abandoned', 'disused'. Rood of the locked door, the sealed
porch. Oh gardener I have surprised you on your lunch break,
your tools silent, your shirt off. You hurry away. There is no mistaking
blood for anything else, nothing else bears the pulse's thread.
I tie it around my tongue, around a twig of yew. These latter days
of canceled amplitudes. Row with them, out to the useful place, the used
place. I will not meet you there. Some things are built to fall into ruin –
Faith is one. The body is another. Stunned credit of the swallow's veer,
the osprey's swoop. What does 'regard' mean, anyway. Observe:
the true nations disgorge their shy beasts, they give them up. *Abducto*,
to lead away. I will be right here, tool or tooth. I dreamt of pain
& then woke into it, a whir of orange wings. Is there something else
that might be done, the concierge asked, solicitously. Her first language
was not my first language, & we both knew this, animals among
the other animals. But my first language was silence. I learned to read
before I knew to speak. Perhaps that was best. Squall
of avian bargaining, the understory, the canopy prevenient in Welsh
light. I wrap my arms around a stone & am not ashamed, or only
a little. The garretfly samples my oils, my sweat. I am a creature of images
towards which the world, like any world, turns. Turns, & vanishes.

On Vision

An Attempt at Reparative Reading

SASHA DUGDALE

I THINK ALL THE TIME and I always thought that everyone else did, too. I still assume this is true, because otherwise what would that look like: an absence of thought? A nothing in the mind, perhaps a cognitive vacuum? Wouldn't a vacuum like that crush the skull from inside? Is that why the ears are placed on either side of the head, two small valves to prevent a vacuum in the event of an absence of thought?

I think all the time, and sometimes I have such great thoughts, they are so intricate and magnificent that they resemble Breughel's Tower of Babel. But I can't ever get them out of me intact. The act of birthing them on paper or in speech reduces them to vague shadows of their former glory. The birthing canal snaps the rudimentary structural props. Like a ship in a bottle, they cannot be pulled back out of the bottle's mouth without splintering and splitting. The rings of Breughel's tower collapse into a nest of sinister sphincters.

If you can't communicate your thoughts then there is no point in having them. That was said to me at university and it is quite true, I suppose. This was my coming-of-age: I slowly got used to having humbler thoughts that were expressible, the apprentice thoughts of a beginner draughtsman, thoughts that were the same reasonable size on the outside and on the inside. I began to understand that the other grander thoughts were follies: unrealisable mental architectures with proportions that couldn't sustain them in the cold world. Slow thoughts! Practical thoughts that proceed in logical order! (My logical thinking is mundane and awkward like a letter to a newspaper.)

But then thoughts are sometimes so delicious precisely because they can't be expressed, their complexity does not permit them to exist. Such thoughts in their dark ingenuity parallel the work of the Soviet paper architects (the followers of Piranesi's Imaginary Prisons) whose baroque and unconstructable designs were an antidote to Soviet planned architecture with its permitted ceiling heights and mandatory rubbish chutes. Paper architecture was the victory of the dreamer over the builder, the idler over the achiever. Paper architecture reminds me of doodling, the pure art of idleness and dysfunction, which claims nothing for itself, but sprouts and spreads across the page, binding, involving itself, convolving, passing its strands through the vulva, allowing the thoughtbabies their billowing form, where they belong, on margins, corporate post-its, backs of envelopes.

When the paper architects Sasha Brodsky and Ilya Utkin were asked for work to show in the USA in the 1980s they decided to make a model from one of their paper designs: a large speckled egg. Brodsky and Utkin asked a foundry to cast the egg. In the past the foundry had produced Soviet statuary and disdained such pointless avant-garde stunt work, but the political tide had turned

and the stream of Lenins was drying up, so they took on the casting of a plaster egg, twelve foot in diameter, in return for some Western goods (so their US dealer Ronald Feldman recounts). The egg stood in the centre of a New York gallery, too large to fit through any of the doors, with a faux-glass-domed roof above it, patterned with etchings and an anxious small figure in black trying to push it: inscrutable birthing device, vast timer, sheer-speckled-stocking, Sisyphean impossibility. It is the utter impossibility of Brodsky and Utkin's etchings which snags the viewer.

I had a Hans Christian Andersen book of stories when I was a child. It was a handsome gift album drawn in the 1970s spindly-saccharine manner, which suited Andersen well. The illustrations were slightly washed-out. There were certain pages I pored over until the paper almost wore through: the ballerina with the spangle stands on one leg in front of a pasteboard castle, reflected in a mirror lake. The castle has a large entrance but a tiny upper floor, like the buildings Giotto painted. The ballerina could never return to her castle, and if forced to do so by the narrator or the *trold* she would have to duck and huddle like Alice in the White Rabbit's house. But no, in fact it was totally impossible, the artist had created such disproportion that the ballerina couldn't ever go back into her own castle unless she grew and shrunk constantly, unless height was not a fixed measurement, but, like weight, depended on where you stood, what force acted upon you. Unfixed, unstable, there was only one way for the ballerina to go: into the furnace with the tin soldier.

I was deliciously vexed by this, it was a deep yearning vexation, like a tickling in the chest. Disproportion! Distortion! It (dis)taught me and (in)volved me: Fritz Wegner's long escalator down into the world of the Fattypuffs and Thinifers; Lucy M. Boston's *Castle of Yew*; lying very silent next to my doll's house with my eye pressed to the door like Alice looking into the garden; the underground bachelor pad of Badger; the underground passages and halls of the rats of Nimh – all the many places of childhood which are larger, more mysterious on the inside than on the outside, just as the child is.

Why do children like small things? Like? What is that sensation? It is not liking, it is wanting to be, to step inside, to inhabit the tiny landscapes inside snow globes, model railways, like Borrowers to inhabit doll's houses, hold pencils the size of matchsticks, tiny glass jars full of beads... Not just children, mice, too: Victorian burglars Hunca Munca and Tom Thumb, stripping bare the doll's house. The feeling is not easy to define. It has something to do with consumption and control, the eyes eating the whole, a counterbalance to a world in which the child has no control, and consumption is limited. But the miniature also offers perfection and harmony, the possibility of realising and entering a flawless ideal, subject to no limitations – a perfection of the imagination, which we are simultaneously drawn into and excluded from by dint of our real physical size.

When the adult manufacturer doesn't understand the importance of perfection then a deep disappointment ensues: at the root of Hunca Munca and Tom Thumb's trail of destruction is the child's disappointment that the doll's house leg of ham is plaster, the knives and forks don't cut, the taps don't turn, the stairs simply stop, the doors don't open. A doll's house must be as good as Gulliver's travelling box and all reminders of fakery, all shortcuts are acts of treason against the imagination, ruler of the miniature land. This tiny land must be impossibly real, that is, more real than reality, which is contingent in childhood and full of adult fakery. It is like being turned out of the garden of Eden when adult fakery is revealed, it hurt like a stabbing pain when the doll's clothes were glued to her chest, and shoddy reality glared into the supernatural glow of the imagination's reality. The fragile controlled world of the imagination cannot be contingent.

Kei Miller's haunting poem 'My Mother's Atlas of Dolls' is rich in meanings and readings, however when I read the poem I was reminded of this tragic potential, the fragility of the miniature world, swollen to enormous scale in the head. In motherhood, we are supposed to be able to control the realm of our family, and the array of miniature figures, dolls from all around the world, each representing an absence, puts the lie to this. In a distortion of the usual it is the mother, not the child, who keeps the dolls impeccably archived on white doilies, longs to inhabit their tiny worlds, the nubs of her children's vast disappearances:

> Unable to travel, my mother makes us
> promise to always bring back dolls
>
> as if glass eyes could bear sufficient
> witness to where she has not been,
>
> the what of the world she has not seen.

('My Mother's Atlas of Dolls', *The Cartographer Tries to Map a Way to Zion*)

In a recent interview on BBC's *Front Row* Miller discussed inspiration. He described how he had filed away the matter of the poem 'in a drawer', and when he began to write his book of poems concerned with 'how we know the world, how we map the world' then the poem came into being. Within the context of the whole collection the mother represents another way (apart from cartographer and rastaman) of knowing and mapping the world in small, serried rows of profound losses. We are not told why the mother can't travel, we must decide ourselves, but the 'makes us / promise' suggests desperation, maternal coercion, even as the line break allows for this desperation to be simply part of 'making' children. Do the glass-eyed dolls teach the mother the impossible, how to travel in death, as the poem suggests? I have been wondering suddenly and sadly whether the poem is now speaking to me as a mother rather than a child: do small worlds of absence teach me how to part with the world? As the mother's world shrinks, the dolls become vaster and vaster, there are more and more of them, the multiplication of their glass eyes.

A long time ago I saw an image by the Russian-American artist Grisha Bruskin from his sequence 'Message 1'. The image haunted me: it showed a boy in the clothes of a young Jewish scholar, simple robes, *kippot*, tasselled prayer shawl, but a pair of huge blue eyes floated in the air where his eyes should have been like twin polyconic projections, two conjoined blue fish. I was reminded of the eyes of my short-sighted elderly relatives, huge in the bottle-glass lenses of their glasses, peering at me in childhood. I could never reconcile the proportions, their kind eyes frightened me. I kept the postcard of Bruskin's image on my desk for years, the boy's disproportionate eyes, saying something important about proportion and sight which I couldn't quite grasp, but I felt, nonetheless. Something that concerned the co-existence of clarity (the childlike illustrative style, perspective-less, unadorned) and mystery (the handwritten words behind him, the enigma of *those eyes*). Now I try to put it into words and it eludes me again: the spectacle of the doll-like child looking out and looking back in, trying to level the two worlds – one clear and bright, the other shadowed, empty – like a lock gate.

I often had dreams as a child which I still remember, and sometimes they return to me in faint echoes when I sleep. The geography of my childhood is quite peculiarly important to this dream. I lived and still live in a village next to a long stretch of downs. A railway runs through the downs, north–south. In my childhood we didn't have a car, so all the journeys I took were on the train. Consequently, I had no idea what lay to the east or to the west along the downs. The north–south axis became practical and known and everyday, the east–west axis withered into non-existence and entered my imaginative life: a miniature land. My dreams concerned themselves with the mappa mundi of this east–west landscape, the towns, their pinnacles, elephants, moons and peacocks, their limitless lives and possibilities. The only way to discover this landscape was by bike so we sometimes cycled off across the fields to advance the edge of the known world by a little mile, always and forever tantalised by bridle-paths leading further into the unknown, towers further off, 'stationary sunlight' over other places.

Now I have a car I travel east–west quite often and that axis is as chartered as north–south. But sometimes, like a revelation, I am driving west and I pass some childhood boundary and something happens, I see differently. For one single second I see the mappa mundi of my childhood again, I see that I am travelling through the land of the imagination, as I travel through the mundane world. The two are briefly in tandem, one overlaying the other, and then the imaginary land is gone again. These moments are hard to describe, they are not mystic, or gilded by spectral light. They come from inside a person, from the life of his or her imagination and not from without. Our vocabulary of revelation is religious and it won't do for these moments of visual overlay, the collision of two perspectives, but nonetheless they are a vision, they enlarge a life, they feel full of ungraspable wonder. I was struck by Marie Howe's poem 'The Affliction' in which the speaker momentarily returns from a place of alienation. It describes so well, so apparently prosaically, the revelation from within, the moment when a lost sight is restored:

> My friend Wendy was pulling on her winter coat, standing by the kitchen door
> and suddenly I was inside and I saw her.
> I looked out from my own eyes
> and I saw: her eyes: blue gray   transparent
> and inside them: Wendy herself!
>
> Then I was outside again,
> ('The Affliction', *Magdalene: Poems*)

Sometimes we see a thing, and then suddenly there is a moment of absolute clarity when we see that thing transformed. It almost appears to look back at us, it changes us and after that moment of transformed vision nothing is the same. In Marie Howe's poem the transforming moments come more frequently after this initial episode, and are the basis of hope. In my dreamlike vision there is a tantalising complexity, a sense of something just-out-of-reach, a perspective no longer open to me, but that I remember distinctly as a sensation, and I am changed by the remembrance of that sensation. It causes pain, a subtle not unpleasant pain like breathing in frosty air, or biting the tip of a finger.

It is common to talk about an insight, meaning a clear and deep understanding (looking into something beyond its surface), but I now see the same word the other way round, in the manner of an optical illusion which flips both ways depending on how you look, pointing inwards, into my body, changing me.

'Send Me an Angel' and other poems

NINA ISKRENKO

translated from the Russian by Anne Gutt

Thirst

Since morning there's been a shake-up in Ur of Chaldea
They change the sheets   They clean the silver
The camels weren't given a drink for the second week in a row
In the water-carrying jug a spider reminds you of the map of the Babylon metro

It's hot The Matriarch brims with milk and honey on the outpost
Now and then the bride is sent with a milking bucket to the roof
The setting sun seeing her thinks I'll beautify the roof too
It's a lot of work to milk the clouds though

She is white-stone Multifunctional Gentle
Muffled in a snow-white bandage to her eyebrows
The slave of sin weary from the road will exclaim Bravo
Dropping beads and sweat on her intimidating pedestal

Come on girl   he's your lord   that is to say the lord of sin
                                    but according to us Aquarius
Come outside as soon as it's dark and at last let him quench his thirst
So that having seen   you   among the pineapples fountains
                                    cappuccino brokers and pizza
The bastard purifies himself and loves you and finds comfort
                                    in sorrow for his mother

10.11.93

Gossip about Dying from Gas

in memory of a poet better than no poet at all

They had a belly-full that evening and the beggars
in their sodden water-proof capes gossiped
smoking slagging off Spanish tobacco
The truck raced over the Nara river
They gossiped that he died like a bull
They gossiped about god   about neurotic dogs about bu-
                     tterflies   about the river freezing-over
The clock forgot its tick-throughtock
flowing down the dry gutter

      I see the plot in perspective
      I'm bored
      I hiccup terribly
      there's no remorse
      in the belly

Like this died the heroes
~~of boundless dull boglands~~
of bloodless blue ballads

They gossip that he perished like an early bird
      I see the plot from the window
      I see and hear feline love

            Turn down the sound   just a bit
            That's fine now   thank-you

From there in the bulging eye of the ~~microscope~~ microcosm
I see a romp on the bed
      they say the story has a crooked thread
      pull it-pull it-tear it off

Is it the bed
              or playing chess?

The matron sits on a cushion
As if it's Chekhov   his mug
Is crushed by the cushion

The Matron plays Salieri
without music   without a hammer without lingerie
oppressing with her heavy rump
punishing the divine image
crushed with a colourful cushion
and with scarlet spots of lacquer

slips down from the wooden nails
and the dune of crimson fatbody
and the herring of hairs
and crumpled sweaty feathers in unclenching hands

But Mozart   they gossiped was one of the sailors

At the stops he borrowed the women
of relief workers and the destitute observing the port decrees
Mozart   they gossiped was a gasbag   and fervid
and told tales of such wondrous places
that his sweetheart's eyes popped out of her head
onto her tiled forehead

against which the maestro so dreamily
                so casually
put out his cigarette

The poor are good at making things up
They gossip about his death   from gas
That's what fate dealt him
             a caramel-cervelat

And although I don't know   Why tell a lie

You yourself are the pest

Send Me an Angel

Send me an Angel   Lord   An Angel...
In the morning I get up and go to the window
Let him notice me there alone
All alone   without an Angel

Send me an agent of Your creative will
                                          and not just rain
A white long-haired one   with wings
                                   and not just rain with snow
It will be difficult for it to get here in the snow and the rain
                                              It's here in an instant
But in the rain or snow not knowing your way around very well
        in the middle of our seemingly monotonous neighbourhood
Not able to distinguish that one in a thousand

But if by the way it's a bright sunny day
that might show how the window glass gleams
You tell it   Not to make haste   not to be nervous
and tell me what to wear

But then I was tormented   That whatever I pick   won't work out
What if it doesn't recognise in my black outline
          my sophistication   my depth   what if it gets frightened
And doesn't see my being at all
And anyway   Who is the Angel?   I hope it's not a man?

I hope that the white   on which it flies
doesn't spoil or melt even if it's not in the fridge
And send it a little earlier
                                   because on my alarm clock
it gets light very early
It's electronic and almost without a tick

So I will hear this white thing arrive   smelling
                        of chrysanthemums rustling as it approaches
and the binary oscillations of the meditations of space
as birds throw into the air minor sixths and thirds `
like fearless soap spheres of sobriety

Peace   Lord   But private peace   domestic sustainable
Ask it   to bring it   in its bosom   It's not heavy
A fragrant shirt front surrounded me   a white chrysanthemum
Mid beige like a piece of soft bread

Everything is stuck up inside me like a piece of soft bread

Lord   it's almost three   But still nothing appears

My time is poured out through a tea strainer
                           slowly   it pours drop by drop
I turn into a medicine glass   I measure by the drop
          And it's already dark in the yard

I'm still standing by the window   Holding back the curtain in my hand
But of course I don't stick it out the whole day   and not every
minute   I need to get the warmth of the family hearth
                                        from a thin ray
to shake a swan out of my sleeve light up the crescent moon under my plait
                                        and clean my teeth
to tie honeyed veins in little bouquets and bunches

I've almost learned by now   almost
          Now the post is delivered and
tea from overseas is brewed under lampshades
Soon   soon it will come   I'll say to it
Without fail I'll say to it   I'll say Look
there's a friendly star burning in the blue heavens
It's yours O my Angel   ever yours
look   look at the unflickering light   of unspoken goodness
Let my prayer be set forth
as incense before Thee
and the lifting up of my hands as the evening sacrifice.

24.03.94

'Place-paint'

on the Ireland Chair of Poetry Lectures

HAL COASE

John Montague, *The Bag Apron* (UCD); Paul Durcan, *Three European Poets* (UCD);
Nuala Ní Dhomhnaill, *Cead Isteach* (UCD); Paula Meehan, *Imaginary Bonnets with Real Bees In Them* (UCD)

IN THE HEANEY memorial issue of the *Irish Pages*, Murdo Macdonald recalls giving a lecture on a landscape by William Johnstone at the 1994 St Magnus Festival in Orkney. Seamus Heaney was in the audience to hear it. Having listened from the back of the room to Macdonald's description of the painting's dual concern with the nature of place and the nature of painting itself, Heaney remarked to Macdonald afterwards that he'd liked what he was saying about 'that artist's place-paint'. There in one go was what Macdonald had been trying to say: '"place-paint" – whether the meaning one takes from this phrase is the painting of place or the placing of paint', or, better still, both together.

The relationship between an artist and place can too often be interpreted in one direction at a time. There's consideration for the 'painting of place', in which 'place' is taken as the abiding subject matter of an artist's vision; a time and a setting that ground a body of work in a world beyond it. And either before or after that, depending on your inclination, there's thought for the 'placing of paint', during which all the artfulness of the art is paramount and the tangible, maybe rather tiresome heft of 'where' and 'when' is put to one side. Most gallery text's still run through this order, sliding from the known facts to interpretative gloss, whilst tourist boards the world over are forever looking to claim a person for a place (witness the little known struggle of Nuneaton to entice George Eliot's readers, which perhaps ended prematurely when one thoughtful campaigner told the BBC, 'she's also a reminder that genius doesn't necessarily grow in beautiful places').

But to claim a person for a place is usually to put things the wrong way round. When the two become inextricable, we're more likely to claim the place, or a version of that place, for the person: Eugenio Montale's Liguria; Jean-Michel Basquiat's New York; John Montague's Tyrone. This personal 'possession' of a place speaks to Heaney's 'place-paint': a lovely muddled-up process that seems both give and take, action and setting, rooted in particularities which it must also radically alter and often depart from. Postcolonial approaches have for decades drawn attention to this process, asking what it might mean if place were reducible neither to an artist's immediate surroundings nor to a work's settings. Might place for a poet be a kind of *method* in which both of these are transformed?

That writers from Ireland are drawn to such questions is, as Nuala Ní Dhomhnaill puts it, 'one of the timeworn clichés about literature in Ireland'. In one version of that cliché, the *dinnseanchas* becomes the archetype for everything that follows, shaping a tradition in which a poem can't stand without a place beneath its feet. It's

understandable, therefore, that the Ireland Professors of Poetry, whose lectures are being published in series by University College Dublin, each have something to set against this cliché: nuanced insights into place, travel and migration, about the palette of experiences which all these can gift a writer, and stories of the often complex relation between a sense of place and a sense of self. It's not that the cliché of place as a thematic preoccupation is simply revisited here (to overstate this theme across wonderfully varied essays would itself be clichéd). Instead, these four poets share wide-ranging thoughts on how to place writing and how to write about place.

Taking as forerunners the 'causeries' of Frank O'Connor and the UCD lectures of Patrick Kavanagh in the mid-1950s, John Montague's essays are perhaps more vivid in their place-painting than the others. They retrace the ground covered in his poetry back to his first collections, *Forms of Exile* (1958) and *Poisoned Lands* (1961), driven by a conviction that travel is always a return, a formative *travail* through which 'among the welter of the world's voices, in the streets, on the airwaves, in the press, you find your own voice'. In order to first recognise and then embrace the odd happenstance of your place in the world, you must first get away from it. This, for Montague, becomes the trial necessary for authenticity ('the holy grail of the artist') to emerge, which is itself a prerequisite to the poet's ability to write of, for and from within their community. To write a poem that can make monuments of homespun familiarities, a poem as remarkable as Montague's own 'Like Dolmens Round My Childhood, The Old People', the familiar must become strange.

Much of this will itself be familiar to those who know Montague's poetry. There has always been a hum of anxiety about being caught either too close to home, surrounded by the 'gaunt figures' of local feuds who 'trespassed on [his] dreams', or else too far away from the action, stranded 'at the periphery of incident', as 'A Welcoming Party' has it. Even the later poems of *Speech Lessons* (2011) are tinged with uncertainties about what a homecoming might mean when home seems a disquieting underworld:

> If I were to return now
> would their friendly shades
> part to receive me,

What Montague's essays suggest is that one way of confronting such anxieties could be with the joy of influence. The second essay presents *The Rough Field* (1972) as an experiment caught happily between the tradition of the long poem in America (*Leaves of Grass* through to *Mountains and Rivers without End*) and the European epic. There's revelry here in simply remaining impressionable. How could it be otherwise? Montague – born in Brooklyn, raised in County Tyrone, schooled in Armagh, returning to America in his twenties 'to explore that great country from end to end', meeting Ginsberg and Snyder on the way, living for several years in Paris and befriending Beckett, then settling in Cork – takes pleasure in the idea of all poetry as a kind of confluence in which the singular voice is a tribute to the voices that have passed it by.

As a model for this, Beckett in Paris remains for Montague the poet-in-exile without equal, riding 'a bilingual bicycle', contemptuous of 'reactionary philistinism' at home and yet when amongst his Irish friends wanting to be 'reassured that the home ground was still there'. Their friendship, recounted in 'Samuel Beckett, Neighbour', provides the backdrop for Montague's encounters with French influences (Jouve, Char and Ponge), which place his own work within a European tradition. Paul Durcan's essays, collected under the title *Three European Poets*, are likewise concerned with the place of literature from Ireland in Europe. They represent an attempt to look past Thomas Kinsella's 'dual tradition', or at the very least to resituate that tradition within a broader continental context. Durcan may be focussed on the personalities, lives and representative works of Anthony Cronin, Michael Hartnett and Harry Clifton but there is always an eye on the literary horizons these figures can open up to their readers. Just as Beckett for Montague, and Osip Mandelstam or Czeslaw Milosz for Heaney, attested to the experience of exile as a fundamental of poetic thought, so for the teenage Durcan making his way into literary Dublin 'the classic Central European artist-intellectual' as represented by Anthony Cronin became the basis for an intellectual, international, politically committed poetics.

For Durcan, Cronin, Hartnett and Clifton succeed as poets in so far as they can be placed within this framework. Cronin's *The End of the Modern World* (1989) patently does. A sonnet sequence split into three parts, written in a direct, conversational tone that is near prose, the cumulative effect of which is the demolition of boundaries that too often separate poetry, history, philosophy, economics and art. The scope is epic but, as Durcan notes, the sonnet form 'frees Cronin from having to occupy the false position of narrative' and what we have instead is Cronin's riotous 'adventures across the mountains and the seas of the history of Western man'. Once again, place is all-important: place as the setting and occasion for dialogue, with travel as the engine of endless intellectual revelations. The sequence rapidly maps a European tour through such revelatory encounters (real and imagined) – walking with Luciano Erba in Salzburg, visiting the grave of Heine in Paris, tumbling through the Vienna of Karl Kraus, Klimt and Schiele. And just as Montague saw distance as the great clarifier of the home country, so Durcan takes the climactic points of Cronin's sequences (sonnet 92 and sonnets 116–122) to be those which 'put Romantic Ireland in her place'. The Stella Gardens sequence performs this act most directly, contrasting Cronin's 1970s home in a red-brick terrace with Yeats's tower at Thoor Ballylee: 'There was supposed to be a Stella Gardens sequence / To put Yeats and his tower in the their place.' The colloquial turn of phrase is here, as in so much of Cronin, the arresting detail. What does it mean to put a place 'in its place'? Is it to place it in a landscape? In a context? Or, perhaps, it is to draw attention to the artful narratives that allow us to acclaim certain places as worthy of attention whilst neglecting others:

> In fact the Stella poems, like extensions
> Projected, never started for the want
> Of money, time and energy, were meant
> To celebrate, as he did, rootedness.

Of course, the 'Stella poems' did begin in some way, we have one here, but they do not seem to be a celebration of 'rootedness'. Their placement within a work that is suspicious of, perhaps even contemptuous of, too easy an attachment to one's roots, suggests that putting 'Yeats and his tower in their place' means in part resolving to do away with verse that straightforwardly commemorates place and to exchange this for an interrogation of how places come to gain their significance, how such significance is gathered through personal encounters, through communities, but above all through the ferocious workings of economics and politics.

Durcan is himself quite openly committed to this line of enquiry. He is, as he puts it, here making a *case* for Cronin's significance as both a break from Yeats's poetics of place and a culmination of an avant-garde modernist tradition. And Cronin, according to Durcan, achieved this with his swaggering faith in the necessity of travel, which allowed his voice to repeatedly inhabit the place of others. Similarly, the essay on Harry Clifton argues that Clifton's 'Benjamin Fondane Departs from the East' is a much-neglected dramatic monologue that gains its energy from its daring willingness to inhabit the other's place (in this case, that of Romanian Jewish poet Benjamin Fondane, who moved to Paris in 1923 and was killed in Birkenau in 1944). And the central essay on Michael Hartnett's *Sibelius in Silence* (1994), argues on similar lines that Hartnett found in this work a way of fusing the poet's voice so intensely with that of his supposed speaker that at times, 'Sibelius is speaking in the voice of Michael Hartnett'. The historic place becomes the ground on which you test the limits of your own given certainties and the dramatic monologue conceals perfectly a back-and-forth, between self and other, of such rapid pace that that it's easy to entirely miss the furious dialogue taking place across it.

Hartnett is supremely in control of such movements and his own reflections on place within *Sibelius* are remarkable for the way in which they seek to widen and intensify the *dinnseanchas* tradition:

> They settled where their dead
> were buried and gave names
> to every hill and harbour,
> names that might become unspoken
> but would forever whisper 'Not yours'
> to mapping strangers;

Here in the poem's opening lines we encounter what Nuala Ní Dhomhnaill has elsewhere characterised as 'a covenantal relationship with the landscape'. In her own essays there is a keen awareness of the weight such a relationship can place on a literary tradition, loaded as it is with patriarchal significance (it's worth noting that Montague's and Durcan's vagrant man of letters is always a man). That patriarchy lies somewhere deep in a named landscape is evidenced by the likelihood that the ceremonial wedding of territory to chieftain (and, by extension, his kin) was the origin of place-naming and therefore of the *dinnseanchas* as well as most other less prominent and celebrated lore. Guided by a mistrust of pastoral traditions which developed from this origin until they sentimentally omitted even the real conditions of a place or the material foundations of their tropes, Ní Dhomhnaill insists upon 'the importance of literary activity *in situ*' which can reclaim literary activity in Irish for popular culture rather than leaving it 'to the devices of the scholarly elite'. In other words, place becomes vital here because it is quite literally *accessible* and tangible in a way that 'tradition' can never be.

This fact is best understood at the level of trope and Ní Dhomhnaill's brilliant final essay provides a persuasive account of how it operates. 'The Hag, the Fair Maid and the Otherworld' begins with the double figure of the maiden and the old hag, both 'as old in Ireland *as the literature itself*'. This slim but critical distinction – between the place and its literature – becomes an opening for the essay's argument: that a literary tradition rests upon a place. On the one hand, then, there is the tradition, from the *aisling* to Stewart Parker's play *Northern Star*, in which the hag is carried out of folklore to serve as a symbol for all manner of things, including Ireland herself. On the other hand, there is the hag as she speaks 'from the mouths of people' who have encountered her likeness or who have grown up surrounded by her presence in local lore. Ní Dhomhnaill is interested in excavating the literary tradition to find its groundwork in this oral tradition, to show that whilst folkloric tropes may well be 'things that aren't there' they are nonetheless sustained and reinvigorated on the level of the Irish language and carried 'mouth to mouth' across the voices of a community. There is a long-standing appreciation of this dialectic in the literature of Ireland; as Patrick Kavanagh's 'Epic' puts it: 'I made the Iliad from such / A local row. Gods make their own importance'. What's distinctive about Ní Dhomhnaill's perspective is its focus on how contingent local folklores are on their particular linguistic surroundings. The making of 'importance' is always a communal act. The significant literary artefact is carried atop the currents of a language and is not something wrought by a poet alone. Unsurprisingly, although her essay 'Kismet' narrates her five years in Turkey as a self-realisation very much in keeping with Montague or Durcan's conceptions of travel, there is a more insistent stress on the *linguistic* dimensions of poetic development: 'Outside the English-language *mentalite* I felt freed to deal with Irish on its own terms. Free of the conflict between my two mother-languages that I often feel when in an English-speaking environment... I came to appreciate my own language all the more acutely.'

Travel is, once again, a way of finding your place. But here that journey has nothing to do with the discovery of an alternative canon and everything to do with a probing of what constitutes every canon: the violent attempt to press the innate freedoms of a language, which moves horizontally across the places it is used, into a fixed shape, organised vertically from the academy down.

Paula Meehan, the most recent of the Ireland Chair's holders to be published, enters this debate firmly on the side of that horizontal movement. There is, as with Ní Dhomhnaill, a desire throughout her essays to ground trope in the personal and the particular, to reconstruct the heritage of the *dinnseanchas* as 'the endured truths of the people who lived in those storied places'. Her essays gain urgency from the holistic, pragmatic environmentalism which so clearly informs them, a position that explicitly connects the loss of environments to a traumatic loss of our linguistic richness: 'some estimates say we lose a language, and its survival strategies, every two weeks'. In search of alternatives to our contemporary disregard for the poetics of place and the place of poetry, Meehan begins by turning to the *Bechbretha*, an obscure part of Brehon Law, which codified civil judgements relating to bees and bee-keeping at a time when honey and wax were prised commodities. The judgements are in themselves fascinating, their very exactitude reminding us that the current mass-indifference to the world surrounding us (sustained by occasional breakouts of guilt-ridden fretfulness) is in no sense natural. In reading them, Meehan begins to envisage a poetics that moves like a bee across a landscape, gathering and giving sustenance, place to place. Ending with a suitably fluid essay that uses 'the language of water' to meditate on source, resource, confluence, influence and the unconscious, the book exemplifies the kind of fresh thinking about place and literature that it also calls for. It borrows its tones and shades from the lexis of the natural world and it then uses this lexis not as a casket of dead metaphors but as an enlivening way of mapping an inner life.

Meehan's essays feel like a place from which to begin a conversation about place and literature in the twenty-first century, one that grows steadily outward from her predecessor's reflections. What's striking are the multiple complications that each poet has brought to bear on this relationship. There is much else across these essays besides, but they do return continually to the places that make up a life and the lives that make up a place: 'place-paint'. In doing so, they provide tender, honest, distinctive accounts of a writer's growth, and they are all resolute that this needn't ever be limited to the mere fact of surroundings. As Harry Clifton put it in one of his first published poems:

> To imagine as I can,
> Beyond the fact of stone,
> A before and to come
> It could never disclose

Three Poems

for Stanley Moss, written in English

YEHUDA AMICHAI

A Blessing for the New Jewish Year

for Stanley and Jane

Even years have religions
And are either circumcised or baptized
Even years have Paradise and hell
And a Year-god.
In Hebrew we wish a good and <u>sweet</u> year
But we now know that sweet and good
Do not always work well together.
If we were Chinese
We would say 'Have a sweet and pungent year',
If we were on a diet
We would say 'Have a sweet and low year'
But then 'sweet and low' is worse
Than sweet and high.
So let's go back and stay happily
In our low-keyed time
Where prophecies and visions and miracles
Are fed into a computer
And thrown up out of it again
And recycled again.

So let's stay in our dull
Imagination-less democracy
Where freedom of speech and will
Have their way
And where you have to choose
Your own personal blessing.

Because blessings are intrusion
Into private life
Like Curses
Only Less Effective.

So my blessing will have
A frame which you will have
To fill out yourself.

I also think of the blowing of the Shofar
This too loud and too wild voice
This obnoxious belch of
Stomach-sick history.
I would rather have

A failed shofar-blow

A shame of the synagogue
A disgrace of the old voice in the desert.

But more like a sigh

Almost a sigh of relief
And nothing but a gush
Of good human air.

So here at your house
We shall watch the horizon
Where the divine accountant
Is sitting over his book of life
And like a good accountant
Let him make little mistakes
In our favour
And sum us up on the good side
Of the book for another
Happy and sweet,
<u>Yes sweet</u>,
Year.

For Stanley and Jane

(my first poem in English)

I woke up early,
awakened by old Jerusalem-time
which my airplane carried
with me and my baggage,
like contraband

I walked on your wooden porch
to and fro like a sentry
guarding some unknown hope.
I walked to and fro on your porch
under your wooden boat
which you had hung from the ceiling
I walked under your boat
I was the sea under it.

Watermill, 21 April 1980

The second Poem I wrote for Stanley in English

This yellow stain of paper
On which I feel raped to write
Has always been intriguing
me, Yellow being the colour
of the Jew-star, of Jaundice
and of the Pope.
But the window is black
The snow outside white
And Innocence is colourless
A transparent see-through thing.
Here in this room
Beleaguered by dogs

And by the Angst
Of being late for planes
Which I hear from above
The clouds,
The bed like a pilot's seat
Ejected into space of dream
Here in your house Stanley and Jane
With both us of forgetting
All about the Art of Poetry
But being great in
The Art of Friendship
A reading together
Of mind with the
Rain Audience applause
On the panes.
And then of course
Back to Israel
To be again in my part
Of the epic *War and Peace*
Constantly in Waiting Rooms
In Peace or War; All the
same doors to open.
Here in this house with
So many thrones to
Change in order not to become king.
But you and I, two
butterflies under the
same glass-pane for a
moment in eternity
alive!

January 1986

Poem for Stanley

Even the swimming pool of Stanley
Is like a big warm heart
With a vein coming in
And an artery coming out.

In the airplane above
People beside the little windows say:
'Down there good people live. We so much
Would like to be with them, down there.'

Their longing adds a pleasant Air-stream,
Which no pilot can measure.

Only the man down there
Who fishes so quietly and writes so quietly
Knows quietly about the depth
Of the ocean
And about the longing above.

July 1984

NOTE

Stanley Moss writes: Yehuda Amichai was born in Wurzburg, Germany in 1924 to an Orthodox family. His grandmother read him Goethe. At El Alamein, he picked up a book from an exploded library lorry, it was the poetry of one W. H. Auden. It hurt him into poetry. He was teaching at NYU when we met at a poetry gala. We hit it off. After a couple of days, I cooked him and his wife Hana ossobuco. Yehuda loved to eat bacon and Kentucky Fried Chicken wings. His family and mine spent wonderfully happy days together, and I some of his last dying days. Yehuda and Darwish went to Stockholm to receive with Rabin and Arafat the Nobel Peace Prize. Netanyahu would be his enemy. He was somewhat phobic about missing planes as Auden was about missing trains, but Yehuda didn't have orgasms in dreams about missing planes as Auden did missing a train.

'Bingham's Ghost' and other poems

LES MURRAY

Frederick Arnall

Son of a fugitive
alderman from Cornwall
my grandfather Fred
took up the shovel
in his early teens
to extract khaki alunite

from an upside-down mine
tunnelled inside a mountain
and send it cascading
down into commerce
as alum, the medicine that
fixed colours in cloth.

Marrying, he moved south
to dig refractive coal,
tarry fossil rock that still
powers half our world
and wrecks lung tissue. Did his,
dead at fifty. Wish we'd met.

Irony of coal, how it
synthesised Nature's hues.
Irony of his tallness
that left him and me
ancestrally Spanish

by the DNA I'd had
checked out in racial times,
not Koori as half hoped
but sherry Castellano
job-hunted long ago
across the Biscayne sea.

Green Catbird

Freckle-headed green
catbird mews its territory
out of mid rainforest.

Both sexes may bound
up from branch to branch
heading for the canopy.

Catbird stays in the bush
paired or single, ready
to play the cripple

tapering off thereafter
into fruit and leaf meals,
telling their green storey.

1917 North

Recruits who brought
their horses from home
left us to ride on them

now we're on track,
creaky saddle, supple back,
to find our way to Beersheba

with a tinny black pan
and a plate of scran
but only dribs of water,

up from Suez
leaving bakers and brewers.
Johnny's waiting in Beersheba.

Tomorrow's to be Gallipoli,
second time, for you and me
on horseback two years later.

We'll gallop through the town
heads or tails or penny brown
as we charge through Beersheba.

Australian Pelican

Stately effortful bird
runs behind its lift
into take off and ascent,

rising out of millennia
with its rigged pink sail
climbing to migration.

Silent collective birds
immersing in unison
drain wrigglings of fish.

Gradually all over
the estuary, pelicans
share themselves singly
post by wharf by boat.

Swallows Returning

Manoeuvre and zip
make a trio of two
swallows just returning
from winterless New Guinea

and now fetching clay
to plaster a cradle
under verandah beams
and nipping the odd spider –

swallows, now tremulous,
now whipping over glass.

Half-Price Hardback

As the bookshops die
in country towns
it's department stores
that stock reader shelves

with detective fiction
with bisex romance
with veterans and war
with cookery and garden

and heaped gifts for children.
This is the culture:
no history but the Allied,
nothing strange. No poetry.

All's preserved slow TV
selling no local memoirs,
no spirit, no religion,
no theory, little foreign

except tourist guides,
no languages at all
only ever middlebrow,
the culture of habitual.

Weebill

Caught a weebill in my gar grille,
bird twice the weight of a hefty beetle.
Only heard it when I left the bush.
If it couldn't home it would likely perish.

Extracted, it whirred off, copse and hollow.
I couldn't drive after it, couldn't follow
its speed among parrots and bigger birds.
I braked, and said a line of words.

All wasted. Its cohort would supply
its brood with forage, if it should die.
If not, it would announce its own homecoming
relearning how to slow and sing.

Pippies

Knotted underwater
through ripple, looking out
until they twist upright
like darkening knife-handles
hardening, keenly split.

Cheery Soldiers

Chokecherry, chokecherry, makin a stand:
I got your little pokeberry eatin from my hand.

Bingham's Ghost

Bingham, alias Lord Lucan
vanished for forty years
without a sign or token
till his title devolved on his son.

Our earlier, flannel-shirt Bingham
vanished from company and speech
just round the time his workmate
turned solemn, with a new tale about him.

Bingham – his forenames didn't last –
had quit bush slog to go scan
for fresh graft down the Hunter Valley.
It had come time to abandon

the cheerless tramp after cedar
logs to fell and float down
the wintry floodwater gullies.
No place for follow-my-leader

but Bingham proved not wholly missing.
Odd times, in moleskins and coat
he'd appear by the Forestry roadside,
moveless, with his pockets pulled out

and patriarchs and other locals
shivered grimly at encounters with him.
Long gone now, he froze many a rider
and silenced whole carloads of revellers.

'The Nut Tree, Time' and other poems

MICHAEL KRÜGER

translated from the German by Karen Leeder

The Nut Tree, Time

The nut tree had to have faith
so as to still its longing for order.
Ten years ago I set a bare root
into the earth, an austere stick,
three years later the first nuts,
puzzling fruit, supposedly
the likeness of our brains.
Everything is sacrificed to order:
childhood, youth, the garden, sorrow.
My brain alone has remained
as disordered as that unruly tree
that cut the ground from under the hazel.
But I needed its shade,
a place to rest and observe,
at the expense of truth, for all I cared.
The empty space is now home to misfortune,
in whose shadow time has made its home,
rapacious time that seizes all for its own,
above and below the earth, in broad daylight.

The Grave

Look, the shining seam
of our footsteps, leading to the grave,
as if the moon had split in two
and shone down, bitter, cold and bleak,
on our path alone and wanted
to know nothing more
of the life in our bodies.
Let us lie next to one another.

My hunger is already given over to the roots,
my thirst to the stones,
my words to the tiny creatures
that make ready for us a bed for the shortest time.

In the Country

So who says that the heavens
are empty and that the man who cowers
beneath them under the scrutiny
of the stars is world poor?
On the doorstep, at home,
lies the passport of the dead,
fetched in by the cat.
Now take an elder switch
to beat the demons into flight
that crouch under the doorframe,
as if they lay in wait for you.

March 2014, under the Apple Tree

This is the hour of those who know all,
who, despite their common sense,
go searching through ashes for bits of proof
that they themselves have burnt.
Disappointed pedagogues.
But the wind takes the ashes,
the wind that consumes all, scatters them far and wide,
over believers and unbelievers alike,
over the beehives that are falling silent,
and over our dazed hearts
that beat on tactlessly into the emptiness.
The ancient art of withstanding contradictions,
so as to take in what is incomprehensible
in beauty has been forgotten, like many a skill,
or is superfluous, like the right to be amazed.
I sit idly under the apple tree
listening to the monologue of the branches
and watching the holy shadows
as they prepare for dying,
long before sunset.

Le Monde, January 2017

For Yasmina Reza

A flimsy, miserable morning
after a long, wretched night.
With honey in my veins I circle the house
like a cat, the wind leans against the gate,
and the sycamore takes pains
to tickle the grass with its spiky shadows.
What should one serve? The truth
and the people. But a man is never
who he thinks he is and, in spite of your work, the one
who comes home is not the one you expected.
He is already inside the house, preaching indifference,
holding forth as if he's out on the square, ice
rattling in his words. There'll be no light now:
we can't find the switch that must be thrown
before we go under.
The little man across the road
with the lantern he hoped was lightning
to make the world legible
like a book.

The Situation

We have been robbed
but we don't know
what is missing.
When we come home
we heave a sigh of relief.
The thief, whom we know,
keeps his secret:
he wants to spare us.

Another Version of History

Wind drops. A dog slinks past,
does not grace me with a single glance.
It leaves behind a path clearly marked
in the snow. The birds are reading earnestly
among the book of beechnuts that lie black
on the white: don't make things too easy for yourself.
From afar the wailing call of a siren,
a sound for charming snakes.
As if this quiet were not enough
to imagine another life.

On Alvin Feinman's *Preambles*

CHRIS MILLER

WHEN ALVIN FEINMAN published *Preambles and Other Poems* in 1964, he already knew, it seems, that his poems were no prelude. They were not a preparation for his corpus but defined the terms debarring him from further poetic composition. The book is at once an allegory/analysis of poetic creation, a genre of which Stevens and Bonnefoy are the exemplary exponents, and an iconic work of aporia or despair. Neither category would matter if Feinman were not a poet of distinction. He is. The chorus of praise that accompanied the publication of *Preambles* included Allen Tate ('"Pilgrim Heights" is one of the best poems by an American that I have seen in many years'), Conrad Aiken ('This is a true metaphysical poetry, a poetry of the whole consciousness... the most exciting thing since Stevens') and Harold Bloom ('This volume may be regarded, some day, as we now regard Wallace Steven's *Harmonium* and Hart Crane's *White Buildings*, as a "first book" that became an essential part of the imaginative consciousness of the age.') I shared their admiration when, finding some of Feinman's poems in Bloom's *The Ringers in the Tower,* I immediately sought out the book. Certain of his lines imprinted themselves on my imagination and have remained with me for more than thirty years. A question then arises why Feinman remains little known, despite the publication of a 'complete poems' in 2016, *Corrupted into Song.** One reason is that his literary reputation was not accumulated over successive volumes; he was, seemingly from the start, a 'dead poet'. Another is the acute difficulty of his poems. This might seem, for a poet publishing in the seventh decade of the twentieth century, par for the course. But it does seem to have been a deterrent, not least because the poems are not allusive and factual annotation is of no assistance. Intermittently returning to these poems and on each occasion pleasurably defeated, I was able to 'open them up' only by sustained study: paraphrasing, listing themes, reading and rereading. Difficult they remain; analysis has to move on to something like acceptance. I have never doubted the merit of Feinman's work, though the volume is uneven. This essay is an attempt to elucidate the poems of *Preambles* and define the nature of their and his difficulty.

The title poem of *Preambles* is in three parts, each of seven unrhymed quatrains. En route to considering its – very representative – difficulty, I should like to cite some prose notes made by Feinman on that subject; they are quoted by James Geary in his admirable introduction to *Corrupted into Song:*

---

* *Corrupted into Song: The Complete Poems of Alvin Feinman* (Princeton University Press, 2016).

Perhaps up to a point in life: there is our overall sense of self, of world (always partly informed) and of language/words as obscurely mediating between them but perhaps falsely committing us when we utter them or they (we, the world) are always compromised into an over-concrete version of each. So the thing would be to say (if one could hear) what language/speech itself wished to say (its own 'intentionality') prior to use (abuse) as sign, where it wanted to go, that poetry in its essence draws on this pure potency of language not simply as sound but that behind the word is the idea of the word, that in this poetry defends us against the world (fixity – already knownness) and our own egotism, wilfulness, or loss of, corruption of meaning: so poetry purges us of the constant crime of speech.

This might indeed seem a counsel of despair, seeking intentionality in something that is, though structured in the image of our own consciousness, by definition non-intentional. Feinman transcends the heuristics of Valéry's 'hesitation prolongée entre le son et le sens'; in his view, meaning is a vulgar or even criminal phenomenon of which pure, non-intentional language could never be guilty – a premise we cannot help but concede. And his prose note illustrates some of the syntactical difficulties exacerbated in his poetry, where the complementariser 'that' appears without clear introductory clauses, and he seems to use argument in Imagist fashion.

The first section of *Preambles* details the way in which mind and language lapse into complacency and repetition:

> Vagrant, back, my scrutinies
> The candid deformations as with use
> A coat or trousers of one now dead
> Or as habit smacks of certitude

What is left is the wreckage of high enterprise: *And the talk // Of memorable ideals ending / In irrelevance.* This is reducible to:

>   All
> Discursion fated and inept
> So the superior reality
> Of photographs The soul's
> Tragic abhorrence of detail.

In the second part, we reach fulfilment, still a heuristic fulfilment, but a clear one: *the child hand in the father's / Rigored, islands tethered // To complicit seas...* And, in one of those moments when Feinman's seemingly awkward meters come together mid-poem in a lyric surge – many of his poems maintain a kind of rhythmic hesitation till the last lines, when everything falls into place:

>   So
> Statues hold through every light
> The grave persuasive
> Candors of their stride.

The third section is, as Feinman's aporia perhaps required, less certain in its movements and themes. Something like epiphany is here:

> The ranged and slackened traffics
>
> Cease A bird in mid-flight
> Falls, let silence, hair
> The credible of touch adventure
> There

In transcribing these, the poet must reduce fulfilment to *of every severed thing // The ecce only.* These are the only things that survive *Where you plead the radiant / Of your truth's gloom* (Feinman suffered episodes of depression). The section begins with, *The stain of dyings seen / On pavements* (the fallen leaves) and ends with an acknowledgement that *the inner* of the human pace is no less *The play of a leaf to an earth.* This places the sexual epiphanies it evokes at the centre of mortality.

The final section of 'Preambles III' is the least rhythmically coherent; it gives, as early as this opening poem, some inkling of the nature of Feinman's aporia. His training was in philosophy, which he studied at Brooklyn College, graduating in 1951 and going on to study at Yale, Chicago and Heidelberg (leaving an PhD dissertation on Kierkegaard unfinished), while the epiphanies to which he aspires seem often to require an unthought and unthinking unity that his mind was trained to reject. So he seems to say in 'Old World Travelogue', in which he compares the immemorial Mediterranean habitat with the New World. Even in the New World, the lyric moments are available, though they have a filmic quality:

> One who strays at a rubbled limit,
> Leans to a river and river-lights,
> Hair-blown, the spell of bridges...

But if we and the poet can *let the will relent*, the unity of man and landscape may prevail:

> So streets encountered in a guileless sun,
> Words shaped to their translated sense,
> A life contrived in a warmer country.

When he perceives in 'Landscape (Sicily)' the locus of history from Alcibiades to the Risorgimento, *Surely*, he says, *I should have wanted / Savagery, a touch icier than physical sport.* If so, he is disappointed, finding only:

> [...] asceticisms grown separate, skilled
> To plump intrinsic endings – the fig-tree's
> Sudden, rounded fingers: history
>
> At the close will cripple to these things:
> A body without eyes, a hand, the vacant
> Presence of unjoined, necessary things.

When combined with *unjoined*, Feinman's *necessary things* are probably as bad as intentionality in language. Certainly, much of *Preambles* is concerned with a search for unities that the mind cannot as easily pull apart as accept – and the *will*, like Time in Steven's poem, will not *relent.* Bloom says of Feinman, 'like Crane, he is wholly a visionary, but afflicted (unlike Crane) with a critical consciousness in the mode of Valéry'.

This is perfectly illustrated in 'Pilgrim Heights', which

opens the second section of the book. Tate is not alone in praising it; Bloom deems it 'one of the most fully achieved and central poems by a poet of my generation':

> Something, something, the heart here
> Misses, something it knows it needs
> Unable to bless – the wind passes;
> A swifter shadow sweeps the reeds,
> The heart a colder contrast brushes.
>
> So this fool, face-forward, belly
> Pressed among the rushes, plays out
> His pulse to the dune's long slant
> Down from blue to bluer element,
> The bold, encompassing drink of air
>
> And namelessness, a length compound
> Of want and oneness the shore's mumbling
> Distantly tells – something a wing's
> Dry pivot stresses, carved
> Through barrens of stillness and glare:
>
> The naked close of light in light,
> Light's spare embrace of blade and tremor
> Stealing the generous eye's plunder
> Like a breathing banished from the lung's
> Fever, lost in parenthetic air.
>
> Raiding these nude recesses, the hawk
> Resumes his yielding balance, his shadow
> Swims the field, the sands beyond,
> The narrow edges fed out to light,
> To the sea's eternal licking monochrome.
>
> The foolish hip, the elbow bruise
> Upright from the dampening mat,
> The twisted grasses turn, unthatch,
> Light-headed blood renews its stammer –
> Apart, below, the dazed eye catches
>
> A darkened figure abruptly measured
> Where folding breakers lay their whites;
> The heart from its height starts downward,
> Swum in that perfect pleasure
> It knows it needs, unable to bless.

The poem is an evocation of the unity with nature that it fails to attain. Speaking of that mystical unity, Bonnefoy says: '*Je suis passé de la perception maudite à l'amour*' (I have moved from accursed perception into love). Feinman cannot move beyond perception, though the intuition of unity is the burden of his regret. As the clouds take the sunlight off the reeds, the body is aware of the fragility of its alien warmth. In a single, winding sentence, its syntactical unity broken into three subjects by three stanzas, the poet attempts to *play out* his pulse or inmost self into the landscape ('play out' can also have the sense 'pay out' or 'unreel'), as though to bind it to the heart. But what it encounters is *namelessness, a length compound / Of want and oneness*. The third stanza of the sentence (fourth of the poem) emphasises Feinman's heredity: *The naked close of light in light, / Light's spare embrace of blade and tremor* cannot help but evoke Crane's

fusion of light, ocean and sexual love in 'Voyages III': 'Light wrestling there incessantly with light'. (For Bloom, 'the dominant influences [in their order of importance] upon Feinman's poetry were Hart Crane, Wallace Stevens, T.S. Eliot, Paul Valéry, Rimbaud, Georg Trakl, and the earlier Rilke'.) That *namelessness*, the otherness of nature, is something of a refrain in *Preambles*. Light is also thematic in his work and Bloom, a lifelong friend of Feinman, recalls him 'chanting aloud Milton's invocation to Book III of *Paradise Lost*'. Here light might be temporality and the impossibility of living in the eternal present of mystic unity. The light steals *the generous eye's plunder / Like a breathing vanished from the lung's / Fever, lost in parenthetic air* – each moment's visual plunder taken away by the moment like an inevitable exhalation, while the *lung's / Fever* specifies in almost Keatsian fashion ('the fever, and the fret') the precarity of warm life on the bare earth.

Like Keats listening to the nightingale, Feinman's attention unspools to a bird, to the hawk that can survey nature while wholly at one with it; the hawk's gaze is an ideal version of his own, as the poet, far from flight, stumbles to his feet, again distracted by his physical self. In a landscape that had, till then, contained only subjectivity and world, he now catches sight of another human being. This *darkened figure abruptly measured / Where folding breakers lay their whites* seems almost to trigger a different sense of unity, that of fellow feeling, yet the last words of the poem repeat those of the third line: *unable to bless*. The figure is, I suspect, a surfer, whose activities are analogous to those of the hawk, in sweeping motion and harnessed to nature; the hawk's shadow *swims* like the heart starting downward from (played out from) its height. No transcendence occurs but its absence is vivid with regret (or denial). Behind *Unable to bless – the wind passes*, I hear Tate's 'Ode to the Confederate Dead', in whose third line, as the 'headstones yield their names to the element', the 'wind whirrs without recollection'.

*

'Pilgrim Heights' opens a section of *Preambles* in which Feinman explores attitudes to nature, and more particularly, to birds and flight. The second poem in this section, 'The Sun Goes Blind', experiments with solipsism, making the entire landscape depend on his perception or even his will: *The sun goes blind against my hand, / I lay the blue surrender of a bay / Down the burning corner of my reach.* He moves the clouds through a *monody* and permits the pines to encroach on *The helmed embankments of my air*. (This is close to Stevens and his Hoon.) We are again, it seems, on the heights overlooking the sea, and again the notion of flight is present in the ambiguous *helmed*: 'steered / helmeted', which, combined with the aerial Brooklands of 'his air', suggest an aviator. But a bird, again *nameless* – and again described as *yellow* in colour like other nameless and alien parts of nature in *Preambles* – finds the poet comically ill-equipped for his volatile aspirations: *too wide to thread to flight, / Too still from bough to fretful bough.* His gravity is borne in on him; his imagination cannot take wing or *play out* into flight. This Sweeney will never go astray:

> Earth presses me in cramped duress – ;
> It is too gross a weight to be

Withheld, to labor forth –
                this
Weight itself of weightlessness.

In 'Scene Recalled', the poet again aspires to flight and specifies the scene: *A time / of gulls riding out / Of the tide going cold at my ankles.* This will be the offshore breeze of evening. But again the poet is belated. His scene is composed as ideal and *Held tall as postponement, / As authority printed to landscape.* The ideal becomes a picture and he resents his own lack of spontaneity, feeling that he should have preferred the more abrasive *flinted salt of occasion.* 'The heart of standing is you cannot fly', says Empson, and Feinman concludes:

You are not the first man who exacted
Of flight it ascend through his shoulder;

Through the copper of nightfall the silver.

The man cannot become the moon and yet, for once, it seems, the moon's flight is consolation in itself.

If flight is the flights of poetry, we reach a kind of decision in 'Solstice', where the hot, rising air distorts the poet's vision of a spire as he sees *the central all / slumped in the sun / breezing itself its mid-day fever.* But he is left with nothing exceptional, unless his own stamping final lines: *only / jackbird sulks in his tree / and the fire of his silence in me.* The Heraclitean destruction of things, the burning up of the solstice landscape by time, brings neither flight nor song.

'Solstice' stands next to its opposite, 'Snow', in which the dialogue with Stevens is again audible. Here we have neither 'the nothing that is not there' nor the 'nothing that is'. Rather, the poem is addressed to one familiar with the neighbourhood that the snow will cover and disguise. The mind cannot cope with the snow's truth, for *the gods give down / Chill unities, the pulver of an under- / Lying argument, assuager // Of nothing nameable.* Instead, solipsistic, it claims the aesthetic unity of a fall of snow for its own, as the duo observe, from within their warm interior (and echoing the pattern of 'Pilgrim Heights'), a fellow-being. Here he is, caught in the confusion of snow-fall and condensation:

The glass that frames this waste
Of contour lames to blur
The baffled figure
To the drift he scurries through
– Blear hazarder. More bold,

The discrepant mind will break
The centrum of its loss,
Sudden and again,
Mistake its signature, as though
Snow were its poem out of snow.

            *

Blear hazarder: Feinman was born in 1929 of an immigrant family of Litvak Jews. His grandfather was a rabbi and Feinman, when working at Bennington College, became known as a reader of Talmudic intensity, a kind of legend: 'two weeks dissecting a single line from one of Pindar's Odes', Geary remembers. After abandoning his doctorate, despite Yale's desire to recruit him, he drifted through various jobs before working in documentary film. But something like depression claimed him: 'He spent years in his room listening to music', wrote his partner, Deborah Dorfman. His friends included Richard Rorty, Harold Bloom and John Hollander; when Feinman was fit to return to the world, Bloom and Hollander recommended that he apply for a post at Bennington in Vermont, where he remained, if I have understood James Geary correctly, until 1994. He died in 2008. Teaching seemed to offer a solution of sorts to his relative sociopathy. At Bennington, he and his poems were idolised and it is strange that almost none of those whom he taught have sought to celebrate *Preambles* in their criticism. In the foreword to *Corrupted into Song*, Bloom brings together the biographical and the thematic in relation to the poem that opens Section III of *Preambles*, 'Relic':

I will see her stand
half a step back of the edge of some high place
or at a leafless tree in some city park
or seated with her knees toward me and her face
    turned toward the window

And always the tips of the fingers of both her hands
will pull or twist at a handkerchief
like lovely deadly birds at a living thing
trying to work apart something exquisitely,
    unreasonably joined.

Bloom first saw this poem in October 1951 and a month later was introduced to the woman, who illustrated the 'action' of the poem before his eyes. Feinman and this 'beautiful, intense young woman', 'though lovers', 'seemed remote from each other', he remembers. And of the poems, Bloom says, 'Feinman has a vision of the mind as a ceaseless activity, engaged in suffering a process of working apart all things that are joined by it', in this contrasting him with Yeats, 'another presence haunting Feinman's poetry'. The poem brings together three of the themes already discerned. Here the birds are both *lovely* and *deadly*. In 'Preambles I', Feinman had written, *Juxtapose that longest vision // A bright bird winged to its idea / To the hand stripped / By a damaged resolution / Daily of its powers.* Flight, then, might be a natural habitation of this world – a natural purpose, uninhibited by reflection – and the sexual a momentary removal from purpose (*A bird in mid-flight / Falls*). The concept, by contrast, though irresistibly seductive, is all too inclined to denominate, part and destroy. The poem thus becomes an analogon of unity, of things *exquisitely, unreasonably joined.* Yet the philosopher-poet cannot be satisfied with a random act of heuristics, and if we return to Feinman's notes on difficulty cited above, we might want to reformulate them and suggest that his poetry attempts to articulate the attitudes or stances that underlie conscious decisions: archetypal attitudes. To articulate them is, of course, in some sense to betray them: *behind the word is the idea of the word*, but the articulation of the idea of the word betrays it to *an over-concrete version of each.* Feinman added: *tempt. to lect., expl. or apologize* (*since poetry is a crime*), concluding, *Poetry itself is a compromise with the ineffable.*

Does this make Feinman akin to the French poets associated with the journal *L'Éphémère* – Bonnefoy, André du Bouchet, and Jacques Dupin (not to mention their colleague Paul Celan) – for whom the poem was impossible: both reprehensible and necessary? Bonnefoy's shares Feinman's hostility to the concept: 'Is there a concept of a footstep coming through the night, of a cry, of the stone rolling down into the brushwood? Of the impression made by an empty house?' But Feinman is concerned with patterns of thought and mood, something both more internal and less specific than Bonnefoy's intended evocation of particulars – from which Feinman shys away (*a bay; some... bird; the literal streets*). Even Geoffrey Hill, 'possessed by a sense of language itself as a manifestation of empirical guilt' that seems close to Feinman's aporia, famously believed that the 'atonement of aesthetics with rectitude of judgement' is possible when 'the poem "comes right with a click like a closing box"'. For Feinman, it seems, the aspiration to articulate the pre-articulate could only betray both parties, while the ambition of some consolatory and conclusive formal perfection remained, by definition, unattainable.

*

If I read it correctly, the third section of *Preambles* is all about the young woman described in 'Relic', the first of three poems so titled. Indeed, to venture an empirical hypothesis, they seem to be a coming to terms with her death. To compound this critical solecism, the hypothesis is that she committed suicide while Feinman was absent in Europe (this is certainly a good way for the critic to make a fool of himself). 'Relic' is immediately followed by 'Three Elementary Prophecies', poems 'For Departure', 'For Passage' and 'For Return'. They lay out a set of attitudes relating to the poet's departure, for which he takes the blame in the opening line of 'For Departure': *You will not want what gives this going speech.* It is one of the characteristics of Feinman's syntax to offer more than one route-map. Here I take him to mean several of the possible construals: 'you will not want this speech / you will not want what motivates this departure into speech / you will not want me, the one who chooses this [speech of] departure'. The second line, *Only as loss the stay of it* must similarly divide: 'you will want that speech only as the prop (the consolation) of your loss; you will want this speech only as expressing the continuity of loss'. The reader (she) is not to *seek a knowledge of this breach / A name of it, as love / The flawless metamorphosis of dying.* But love is also *membered... / To your days' held mine* – again an ambiguity; her days held his, but the apostrophe makes a *mine* of her days, with the further ambiguity of potential riches / explosion. The final two stanzas seem to detect hope only in change:

Only this presence destined
As a weather from its source
Toward broad or violent unleashings
Fables of the suffered and the joined

The rest unnumbered and devoid
A wind that will not move or pass
Rain tangled to a ruin, to
A season's felled, forgotten root.

'For Passage' is barely more conciliatory: *Nail your will to the yellow fallings / Of your days, as tragedies slip / Their herald warnings through their acts.* But 'For Return' suggests a process of recovery: *There love will touch where your energies begin.* If I am right, the next four poems – in which the influence of Crane and Eliot is at its clearest – memorialise her death. 'What Land' seems to borrow its title and some of its metaphor from the Senecan epigraph to Eliot's 'Marina', but focuses on a drowned body. 'That Ground' must be a grave: *Never will it be possible to illumine that ground, / But know how her breathing / Shapes the hapless arms of trees.* 'This Face of Love' seems to combine memories of sexual *petite mort* and her death. In one of Feinman's most mysterious poems, 'For the Child Unanswered in Her', he presents a vision of her childhood but finds the loam is no mother. A wonderful image links aesthetics to the breastfeeding babe and the human artery:

– O listen,
The splendid throat of every column
Aloud in the beating nipple.

Bridgelessly lit as the seed's leap,
Convene your gaze to the Mortal Brow
Always near, always unable to return your wish.

Does the capitalisation make a god of man's rationality, creating a contrast between the natural miracle of conception and impossibility of perfect empathy? The coinage *Bridgelessly* and the Latinate *convene*, used transitively with *gaze*, record the influence of Crane, who is still more present in 'Relic 1' and '2' – *your trackless survival of eyes* – though I also hear the Valéry of 'La fileuse' in the last lines of 'Relic 2':

As by gracious rain, frail windows,
Your eyes' help for the bitter green of the leaves.

These poems are indeed reliquaries. Perhaps 'Relic 3' tells us that hers was a suicide like Crane's. The section ends with 'The End of the Private Mind', which also marks the end of the 'biographical' in my hypothesis; it is, I think, her mind that is at an end, in the form, perhaps, of a stone grave marker:

The death of it was generous,
as it lived, only silly, and yet
not sillier, for Care
like an empty sleeve...
                    For Care,
a shy grass quite in the cracks.

We remember that, in *Macbeth*, 'sleep... knits up the ravell'd sleeve of care, / The death of each day's life'. Feinman writes of this death... *it was not / obscure, but public as nails*, evoking the expression 'dead as nails', a variant of 'dead as a doornail' and used, for example, by D.H. Lawrence. 'Shy grass' is one name for 'Mimosa pudica', which folds away from touch. *Care* alone is left among the stony public monuments, as though the public face of death were an intolerable intrusion on a private life and private griefs.

*

Section IV of *Preambles* is the most objective exposition of the attitudes of mind that Feinman analyses – so much so that the opening poem, in six parts, is called 'Statuary'. These are to be *Tags, or stations, every bold / Approximate of everything, like leaves / The only pulp of what an autumn ought to be.* But they are also, as such, revelations; epiphanies given final, petrified form (*So statues hold through every light...*). In the second poem, the human mind may come to a permanent halt, *Gripped to an immortal truth* and becoming an *iron / Archangel of its parable.* But the world will continue unheeding. The third, 'Portrait', speaks once out of the stillness of the image, but cannot repeat the feat. The fourth, 'Sentinel', rehearses a monomania such as '2. All of this' describes: *...an ignorance / that stands as though it were a center.* The fifth poem, 'L'Impasse des deux anges', refers to a famous cul-de-sac in Paris, under whose sign Paul and Nusch Éluard were photographed by Man Ray. It formerly linked with rue Jacob, which perhaps brought to Feinman's mind another monument of the 6e arrondissement, Saint-Sulpice, with its Delacroix mural of 'Jacob Wrestling with the Angel':

Where two contrive one slant
Of combat locked, a boldness
Blind to the fury of its formal light.

He concludes: *Regard these two, perpetual, firm, / Closed in struggle that cannot bend.* It is hard not to see this poem as symbolising Feinman's aporetic genius, in which the semantic requirements of poetry meet an equal and opposite formal resistance.

*

The final section of the volume opens with another of Feinman's most exalted performances, 'November Sunday Morning'. In giving the poem here without its final verse, which was excluded in *Preambles*, but reappears in *Poems* and *Corrupted into Song*, I directly contradict the poet's wishes, unable to perceive the relevance of his addition:

And the light, a wakened heyday of air
Tuned low and clear and wide,
A radiance now that would emblaze
And veil the most golden horn
Or any entering of a sudden clearing
To a standing, astonished, revealed...

That the actual streets I loitered in
Lay lit like fields, or narrow channels
About to open to a burning river;
All brick and window vivid and calm
As though composed in a rigid water
No random traffic would dispel...

As now through the park, and across
The chill nailed colors of the roofs
And on near trees stripped bare,
Corrected in the scant remaining leaf
To their severe essential elegance,

Light is the all-exacting good,

That dry, forever virile stream
That wipes each thing to what it is,
The whole, collage and stone, cleansed
To its proper pastoral...
                    I sit
And smoke, and linger out desire.

The volume ends with a clear tribute to Valéry and his variants on 'Narcisse', Feinman meeting his own reflection by the lakeside and playing his own variation on *'le ride me ravisse au souffle qui m'exile'* (May the ripple ravish me away from the breath that exiles me):

– How we exchange circumferences within
The one footfall that bruises us asunder.

*

Feinman's goal, of an impersonality of inspiration such that language itself seems to be writing the poem, is clearly at odds with the epiphanies that he is willing to recognise, while his analysis of archetypal states of mind is not one that a wholly heuristic compositional method could be expected to throw up. Bloom cites Valéry, who adduces all the sensuous evidence of the outer world to illustrate the changing states of the inner one, but Feinman is rarely a sensuous poet and, though images stand for thoughts, as they do in the early work of Bruno Tolentino, the very images are abstract. He sometimes flinches from the substantive, preferring to create nouns from adjectival forms – 'those starks', 'barrens' – while his adjectives often reflect an inner necessity or essentialism rather than attempting to reinvent appearances. Feinman's is a philosopher's and a philosophic poetry that seems, precisely for that reason, to privilege the naïve and unreflective because they escape his burden of intellectual despair. In 'Visitations, Habitats', the poet asks for *Currencies of sense which can stay... / ... as / ... battle-scenes detain a color and a face // Outside the campaign's vigor*, citing an example of such permanence: *the arrow / Of your kiss uniquely blinds / Through the bright sorrows of all our days.* But he concludes with... *the fear that broken / Splendor breaks us where we live, the life / We gather to our life we never own at all.* Love might, again, be our deliverance, but even in this he cannot believe, evoking the Humean refutation of Descartes's *ergo sum* in reference to *those faces / Which resume each morning separately*; each individual separately evolves minute by minute away from each previous self (or love). What is astonishing, then, is that out of such asceticism any poetry was ever allowed to grow. 'We lost lots of fine poetry because of Alvin's curious attitude', writes Bloom, saying (in *The Ringers in the Towers*) that Feinman sought to write 'the last possible poem, a work that takes post-Romantic consciousness so far as to make further advances in self-consciousness intolerable'. My own analysis makes this aporia less a matter of Bloom's 'Ananke' than of the mutual repulsion of philosophical analysis and a formal heuristics – but it should be said that Bloom has, in addition to his own authority, that of Feinman's lifelong friendship.

Since for many readers this will be a first encounter

with Feinman's spectral muse, I should like to end with a poem that, while self-indicting, affords, perhaps, the faintest glimpse of a different end to his career, a moment of impersonal acceptance expressed in a beautiful lyric (from the which the Complete Poems takes its title) – 'True Night':

So it is midnight, and all
The angels of ordinary day gone,
The abiding absence between day and day
Come like true and only rain
Comes instant, eternal, again:

As though an air had opened without sound
In which all things are sanctified,
In which they are at prayer –
The drunken man in his stupor,
The madman's lucid shrinking circle;

As though all things shone perfectly,
Perfected in self-discrepancy:
The widow wedded to her grief,
The hangman haloed in remorse –
I should not rearrange a leaf,

No more than wish to lighten stones
Or still the sea where it still roars –
Here every grief requires its grief,
Here every longing thing is lit
Like darkness at an altar.

As long as truest night is long,
Let no discordant wing
Corrupt these sorrows into song.

'Come, gentle night': here at least it seems that, though in a world of suffering, the moment of peace can be both eternal and recurrent. But in that world, the lyric tells us, the only anathema is song.

'Holiday with the Knudsens' and other poems

BENJAMIN NEHAMMER

Of Where to Begin

A man offers you a dry red wine
directly from the bottle. You can
smell the knowledge on him.

You tend not to show your best
impressions to strangers. They may
prefer the fraudulent if

illustrious wave, the image as
surface, this glass stained yellow
to be passed and reflected

in sickly overcast. Knowing
the kind of food they serve here,
you turn down the brownish olive,

the crude rhubarb pie, that thing
you were certain held cilantro.
Then he comes back,

the waiter, leaving his tip
for you to divine. It occurs then
that the eye catches itself

in the very act of seeing.
You realise the ocean is
any number of reflections.

Palm Trees

These beaches here: they sang
Last night your praises.
They broke among the waves,
Blathered away with each fall

And rise of their blue thought.
Between their lines, your face
Billowed like a sail –
Between their winds, the word

Spoke something about God,
About His wandering here, also,
To sleep long nights through the cold.
These flashes of sand are His,

If you believe in that sort of thing,
And even the forlorn view of sandals
Spooling on the water's edge.
Yet you are known only to yourself

As someone frail and angry; you
Recall slow shapes of palm trees
Turning greens to new golds;
You recall yourself in their shade.

The Year of Song

He is away beneath the bridge
because the cops can't get to him
and neither can you. Stark, freezing
blade – his flaked collar shattered
to its core – he holds one shoulder
as though letting go would split
the bone once more. This crazy
town we're having, drowning
the noise of life ebbing from
his bluelit corpse. Yet, getting up
(and this is where your story begins),
the man bares you his nakedness.
He wears nothing but the soul
of the boy whose life he took,
t shirt in relentless dark, purple

reds like clouds rekindling lakes:
Old Joe, truckstop gasoline
peddler who wore his faith across
the chest, who let down a window
and called, Get outta there you
crazed kid you'll freeze to death.
A cut moon slips his gold
light past and shows
his skin lit through, a yellow
like old paper, like the sun.
Soon the man refires, his nerve
back to life. Go to hell, he says.
He snaps his fingers like snow
flung to jump and pivot in the air,
his toes a wild elderberry, blackened
to the vein. (You did not see
the abandoned lots of dandelion,
the rows of cars turning eastward
through barely lit evenings.)
He stumbles, gets up to lean
on the world. Go to hell, he says.
But he'll never drop, you think, we
all will die before he gets that cold.

Holiday with the Knudsens

The finch is far out now,
though it is too late to assume
any normalcy of things as
some predetermined distance.
The finch never leaves
much behind – though it returns
for whatever it was. I was
once here as well, present
for the return of finches, all
yellow-breasted yolks
impossibly alive between
this coldly lit summer house
and some purplish distance.

'Sheeple' and other poems

TAMAR YOSELOFF

Snails

Withdrawn from toxic sprays, deadly beer,
they aestivate, motionless, in grave homes,
a vital straitening;
                        holed up for days,
ignoring the radio, the funereal newsreader,
we dine on their gummy bodies, tight knots
we prod from shells with little forks
then dip in garlic butter, dangling them
before our mouths
                        leaving only
a hard case, an empty offering:
the spiral's apex – a whirlwind uncoiling.

Climacteric

Now I arrive, late
on a frozen sea. Distant glints
mark habitation: a barren
hillside dotted with breeze blocks
where happiness smacks of youth.

Here I'll make do, reinvent myself
from scraps and songs
while poised on a balcony,
a distant marble goddess.

I might as well dance
to appease the monsters.
Once they demanded respect;
now they're old, a bit frayed,
they suck light, rust the past.

Sheeple

The train slows to a halt in some shire
or other. The heartland. Lower Slaughter.

Two of them, like cumulus on stilts,
perform a moonwalk in reverse, step

by courtly step, before they charge,
almost lifting off, crashing head to head

and then again, hard-wired to the bunt.
Wars of the flock? Dick fight? Tense détente?

What ticks in their spongy brains?
The rest chew cud, footrot rooting them,

the green and pleasant place of no escape.
They ruminate in marshy gas, while all the birds

of Oxfordshire and Gloucestershire
feast on their creep.

The Treasury of Alonis

To pine means to yearn, this is what we do,
on a hill above the sea where Romans prayed
to equinoctial deities.

What do we mean when we say we have faith?

At the temple site the ditch fills with plastic bottles, Coke cans
for our descendants to excavate:
will they conclude this was the start of our decline?

Divers sweep the sea floor where a merchant ship sank,
cargo intact: amphorae packed with garum. We stuff our mouths
with *boquerones*, wipe our salty lips, call the waiter for more wine.

To pine is to lament what we don't have, what we lost –
trees cling to the cliff edge,
our fingers are sticky with resin.

What do we mean when we say we've lost our faith?

The goddess could occupy a pocket, fit a hand;
her owner kept her close. Only her head survives.
Her hair is waved like the sea. In her glass case we see our reflection.

And in this case, the bones of a soldier, plain as the grave.
His remains can tell us how he lived, how he died.
Can we excavate his soul?

The women wore amulets of gold, element of eternity.

To pine is to ache, to waste away.
It isn't skin that keeps us whole.

From the Archive

Issue 145, May–June 2002

SUJATA BHATT

From a contribution of six poems
alongside 'Only the Blackest Stones'
and 'Good Omens'. Fellow
contributors to this issue include
Marilyn Hacker, John Gallas, Robert
Gray, Moniza Alvi and Valerie Duff.

WHAT IS EXOTIC?

for Hasso Krull

Sweden is exotic –
and so is all of Finland.

Whortleberries certainly are.

Estonia is exotic –
and so is the Estonian word
for lizard: *sisalik*.

But the lizard herself
is my sister - those hot afternoons
when she comes indoors
            to hide -

'My Blue Period' and other poems

REBECCA WATTS

Finds

I could say: dragon's tooth,
philosopher's stone,
gold dust

but I'm clearing out the car on trade-in day

so I say: black toggle off your duffle coat,
pebble (I forget where from),
thin covering of sand.

But, but... says a tape I've never listened to,
which predates me and is labelled in your
earnest hand: BLUEPRINTS / NIGHT.

Interns

Five days out of seven we go to the Work Room. We work on Projects.
We turn on the computers cheerfully and tap the keys. We exchange stories
but not about our Projects, to which we've been specially, individually assigned. Now and then
He descends and, rather than gliding from the building to unspecified, important places,
enters the Work Room like a blast of liquid nitrogen only talking. We tap cryogenically
in time to a collective, unvoiced *Don't pick me*. Whomever He picks
we all listen to the Brief with our best listening – as a rabbit
sluiced in 1200 lumens of lorry light on shuddering tarmac might be said to be listening.
When He exits the air unpresses itself from the ceiling and slowly expands until it once again touches all
     seventeen corners of the Work Room,
where we tap the keys cheerfully, grateful for the opportunity.

Daffodils push through in the mild first days of January,

causing my colleague to say 'too soon –
they'll regret it next week when a hard frost sets in'.

And yet, for them, *early* and *late* don't mean;
they do what they do while conditions allow; and if to him

they symbolise disappointment or failure, or
the bathetic hubris of the eager,

they also show how nature deals not in *ought*
but *is* – the blip of green or yellow breaking up black

soil, perhaps not making it.

My Blue Period

No one could create great works
in those pyjamas, you said.

It's high time you got up
and got out, you said.

I'd love to tell you how
I did get out

        as out as out could be

               with all my clothes off

    walking away from this

          too too solid ground

the very minute the sea

      melted over that groyne

the very spot

      where I'd left my stuff

        (even you wouldn't have predicted it):

and now I feel much
like my phone, which lies

comatose beside
me in a tub of rice.

Worship Not the Object But the Thing It Represents

Studio Apprentice

Who is it I love? I gaze through layers
at The Virgin Mother and The Infant Christ,
but here's *our* Mary with her child wrapped
in silks (Egyptian blue, verdigris), and
tiny boats all busy on the sea behind
them. And then in her eyes (burnt umber,
yielding as clay) there's Maria, who barely
moved the whole time we sketched, and never
complained, but soothed and shushed and dandled
the baby so it smiled for us again.

Novice

The trouble is the doll – so hard and so
unnaturally shiny! *Here is a*
focus for your love of Christ, they said, *to*
practise your devotion on. But its knees don't
bend and its stuck face smells like a workshop.
Once I saw a statue of the Christ child,
his chubby legs rendered so soft you could
pinch them. And in the paintings his skin's as
kissable as a peach. Like love made flesh.
It's fine here but I miss my family.

Scholar

Yet they come, like bailiffs, with their roll
and index, their hammers for the printer's
plates and their buckets of fire. To purge
a man of sinful thoughts, burn paper?
An idea is already smoke; it crosses
channels, regardless of ink. And
freedom is the stuff of days: men's minds
cleave to it as monks to a rosary.
Poor faithful puppets: they knock and knock.
I memorise the contents of my books.

Time Away: Louis MacNeice in America

TONY ROBERTS

Time was away and she was here
And life no longer what it was.
The bell was silent in the air
And all the room one glow because
Time was away and she was here.

'Meeting Point'

IN HIS PROJECTED *Countries in the Air* Louis Mac-Neice had been keen to explore 'the corroborations and refutals of my myths, the frustrations and illuminations I have found in various travels'. His American experience provided much fertile ground for this. MacNeice's brief working visits there, while successful professionally, led to something of an attenuated romantic disaster. His relationship with Eleanor Clark, the American writer whom he met in New York in 1939, overshadowed his engagement with the country. It did, however, inspire some fine poetry and, in his letters, a vivid self-portrait of a poet conflicted by love and duty on the eve of the war.

MacNeice's life until that time had been one of public success and private heartbreak. He was born in Belfast in 1907, to a clergyman father and a mother he lost in 1914. Prep school in England led to a Classical Scholarship to Marlborough College and subsequently Merton College, Oxford, from which he gained a first in Classics. He published his first collection of poetry, *Blind Fireworks*, in 1929 and the following year married and took a post as an assistant lecturer in Classics at Birmingham University. Although his marriage had produced a son, Dan, in 1934 he was divorced two years later and MacNeice moved to Bedford Women's College (London University) where he taught in the Greek Department. He published regularly throughout the decade: fiction, a translation of *The Agamemnon of Aeschylus* (1936), *Letters from Iceland* (1937) with Auden, his entertaining *Modern Poetry: A Personal Essay* (which drew Orwell's scorn on his generation of poets) and a second poetry collection, *The Earth Compels*, in 1938. After a visit to Barcelona in December of that year, MacNeice turned his attention to the writing of *Autumn Journal*, to his study of Yeats and to America.

To that end he asked T.S. Eliot's help in organising a short reading and lecture tour for the spring of 1939. Letters went out to a number of prestigious institutions. Writing to Wellesley College, Massachusetts, Eliot described him as 'one of the best of our younger poets, whose work is I am sure known to you'. MacNeice left immediately at the end of Easter Term at Bedford College and in New York he was met by his ex-wife, Mary, and her husband, their one-time lodger. His first lecture, at the state college in Pennsylvania was well-received, he remembered in his unfinished autobiography, *The Strings Are False*. His host told him: 'They gave you a big hand. They usually only do that for an orchestra.' Other readings at Princeton, Harvard and Wellesley, although successful, failed to underwrite his expenses. Nevertheless the trip provided useful academic introductions and included a reunion and reading with Auden and Isherwood.

At a *Partisan Review* party MacNeice met Eleanor Clark, a twenty-five-year-old left-wing, Vassar-educated writer, divorced from one of Trotsky's secretaries. In contrast to Clark's political commitment, although also left-wing in his sympathies, MacNeice was too sceptical, too much of a lifelong outsider to embrace Marxism, Communism or any ideological constraint. As he was to express it in a later letter: 'I am trying to develop [a world-view] but I am damned if I am going to swallow Marx or Trotsky or anyone else lock stock & barrel unless it squares with my experience or, perhaps I should say, my feelings of internal reality.'

Returning from the tour on board the Queen Mary on 21 April, 1939, MacNeice initiated three years of correspondence with Clark when he wrote breathlessly, 'So few people have both beauty <u>&</u> intelligence <u>&</u> a conscience <u>&</u> gaiety but you seem to, darling.' Clark on her part endeavoured to keep some distance between them emotionally, though MacNeice bombarded her with lengthy letters which attempted – festooned with 'darlings' – to erase it. He was also keen to breach the 'Hindenburg line... which you were very reluctant to stop defending'. This physical aspect became a leitmotif of his letters, just as his worry about 'suffocating' her in his effusions (while continuing to do so). He did not completely lose his senses, however. He was, for instance, wary of sharing her commitment to revolution, wondering about the 'internal capacity for revolt' of the 'lower classes'.

Arriving home, he reported 'several painful scenes & been made to feel very conscious of moral irresponsibility etc'. There would be disapproval if he were to return to America, he knew, and he cited the experience of Auden and Isherwood as a warning. Still, he was 'sick of this place' by early May. To alleviate his 'American fixation' he asked Eliot's help again, this time in obtaining a semester's academic appointment, although later Mac-Neice stood in two minds about a lecturing job ('They all work so hard that I am not sure I shouldn't prefer hanging about and living by visiting lectures and journalism'). Subsequently he was offered a 'Special Lectureship in Poetry' at Cornell University from 12 February to 3 May (for $2,000), with added lectures elsewhere. The offer enhanced his emerging reputation after the publication of *Autumn Journal* in America in January 1940. The dust cover of *Poems 1925–1940*, published by Random House, referred to him as 'one of the leaders among England's younger generation of poets'.

MacNeice defended England when Clark wrote that the country was 'doomed'. He was not at all convinced by the prospect of war and anyway, as an Irish citizen he was exempt from conscription. What worried him had more to do with the endgame: 'I do hold that morally the British Government ought to check Hitler, there will be so little morality in it by the end of it that I don't feel very inspired to have my legs shot off to bring about that a Europe which is now say 80% rotten should be 85% rotten, supposing H. is checked, instead of say 89% supposing he isn't.' To his mentor, Professor E.R. Dodds, MacNeice wrote on the 13 October, 1939: '"Destroy Hitlerism" but what the hell are they going to construct?' He was sure of one thing: that a trip to the United States was necessary 'in order to clear myself up emotionally. Three months would solve the question of E. one way or the other'. The following month he vacillated, writing to Dodds, 'I am beginning to think this may be my war after all.' Despite the fact that 'there is plenty wrong with the British Empire & especially India', he hoped perhaps that events would right wrongs even if the government lacked the will.

In December MacNeice's other option closed. He had held hopes at the prospect of appointment to the Chair of English at Trinity College, Dublin, his application supported by T.S. Eliot and Professor Dodds, (later to be his executor). When he heard that he had not been chosen for the post, MacNeice turned his attention back to the burning issues of romance and responsibility. Christopher J. Fauske put the matter bluntly in *Louis MacNeice: In a Between World* (2016): 'He would return to the States in January 1940 motivated by an intense ambivalence about the war, an inability to find permanent refuge in Éire and a desire to see and seduce Clark.' In his autobiography MacNeice addressed his prevarication as follows: 'I felt I was not justified in supporting the war verbally unless I were prepared to suffer from it in the way that the underprivileged must suffer. But I was not yet prepared to do this, so I had made use of certain of my privileges to escape for a little to America. I had an especial reason for wanting to return to America, but apart from that I thought I could think things out there, get myself clear before I went back into the maelstrom.'

The 1940 trip was starred with ill-luck, though the lectures went well. Their subjects included Yeats, Eliot (at Vassar), as well as the poems of Auden, Spender and himself. He also lectured on 'Since the Victorians' at Skidmore College and 'The Younger English Poets' at Bennington, where he was paid $25 for a talk which necessitated an arduous journey involving two buses and a train.

Disaster struck in July when MacNeice had to be hospitalised in Portsmouth, New Hampshire. He endured an emergency operation for peritonitis, followed by a near fatal infection. Recovering, he was taken to Clark's mother's house in Roxbury, Connecticut, to convalesce. There he stayed for several weeks. In mid-August he wrote to his ex-lover, Nancy Coldstream, of perhaps migrating to the USA 'unless there is a social revolution in England which makes everything new'. He had grown attached to this country, he decided, though that attachment was to weaken as his relationship with Clark failed to develop. Meanwhile, he began 'pouring out poems in an unprecedented state: five ballads, 'Jehu', 'Picture Galleries', 'Plurality', 'Autobiography' and 'Province' among them. No wonder he wrote giddily to Clark, 'I have written

ELEVEN since coming here; what do you think is wrong with me?' *Plant and Phantom*, published in 1941, collected these American poems with others. For the reader, the reward of MacNeice's American time is to be found in the poems he composed there, poems which reflect his feelings about the cost of neutrality, the fate of love and the coming conflagration of the world order.

One was 'Bar-Room Matins', written in a 5th Avenue New York apartment. It imitates the tough-mindedness of hard drinkers, its prayer satirising the hypocrisy of everything from church to media and ending with rather harrowing foresight: 'Die the soldiers, die the Jews, / And all the breadless homeless queues. / Give us this day our daily news.' 'Refugees' – written around the same time –shows insight into the lot of immigrants arriving in New York. The poem is informed by MacNeice's compassion and by his recent experiences of fellow passengers at sea:

> Thinking, each of them, the worst is over
> And we do not want any more to be prominent or rich,
> Only to be ourselves, to be unmolested
> And make ends meet – an ideal surely which
>
> Here if anywhere is feasible.

Something or nothing may turn up, but for these refugees the known world has gone. As he neatly concludes, 'they still feel / The movement of the ship through their imagination / The known and the unheard-of constellations wheel.' 'Exile', another poem of 1940, seeks to hide the 'inhuman night' after such recognition:

> Knowing that in Europe
> All the streets are black
> And that stars of blood
> Star the almanac

'Picture Galleries' reminds us 'of what we always / Would rather forget – that what we are or prefer is conditioned / By circumstances, that evil and good / Are relative to ourselves who are creatures of period'. And this is not the time or place for lasting love. The fine poem, 'The Closing Album', from August/September 1939, ends:

> And why, now it has happened,
> Should the atlas still be full of the maps of countries
> We never shall see again?
>
> And why, now it has happened,
> And doom all night is lapping at the door,
> Should I remember that I ever met you –
> Once in another world?

Neither can the bucolic pleasure of neutrality, of an 'Evening in Connecticut', hold the world and its war away:

> The lawn a raft
> In a sea of singing insects,
> Sea without waves or mines or premonitions

Despite the beautiful September and the katydids, Nature is no guarantee of continuity. The coming fall evokes not quietness but 'the fall of dynasties'. 'Only the shadows longer and longer', the poem ends. As with 'Jehu', the mood is prophetic of 'the flood tide' coming. And consequently in 'Cradle Song for Eleanor' (which 'reads like a valediction as well as a benediction' as Edna Longley noted) MacNeice's protective injunction is to:

Sleep, my darling, sleep;
 The pity of it all
Is all we compass if
 We watch disaster fall.

The best that can be done is to slip the moment, to take time out of the coming war, as MacNeice and Clark do in the famous 'Meeting Point', which he wrote in late April 1939. It is 'a kind of love poem in the third person', he told Clark and, transmuted into art, the expression of MacNeice's feelings is highly seductive. In the reality of his letters, the romantic immediacy is raw. That of 21 May 1940, written from Ithaca New York, is the most revealing and most devastating of MacNeice's side of their correspondence. Certainly sexual frustration plays a part in his defence of his supposed 'awful lack of curiosity about the world': 'once again you seem to forget the distracting effect sex has on one (in situations like mine at the moment)'. In this angry letter MacNeice attempts to dispel 'this little pixie myth about me' Clark was supposed to share with her sister: the belief that he has been sheltered from the world and has kept himself aloof from others. In fact, an ironic reserve does seem to have characterised MacNeice. His friend John Hilton later wrote: 'Meeting people face to face he was apt to make too clear that he was treating them – head thrown slightly back, eyes quizzically narrowed – as specimens, bearers of the potentialities of the race.' Hilton generously interpreted this watchfulness as self-protection.

In that letter to Clark, MacNeice presents himself as a 'peasant who has gate-crashed culture'. He is, in his own words, able to identify with common people, being one of them. He is aware that he may give the impression of being stand-offish, of being 'inhuman' but, 'I couldn't keep on feeling on behalf of other people. And so I got this detachment or aloofness or whatever it should be called but if you think I am aloofness to the core & can't see behind what was only a protective crust, you are, darling, more short-sighted than I should have expected.'

The letter may have cleared the air, but their relationship was doomed. Christopher J. Fauske concludes that, 'Ultimately, she was less interested in him than in what he stood for, and he was more interested in her than in what she stood for.' What MacNeice might have stood for, however, was the nub of the problem for Clark. When he wrote: 'The trouble (& the glory) about being in love with you is that I see you against the world,' she replied, 'I don't see you that way.' She was beginning to find it difficult to see him in any way. What he offered was the wrong kind of commitment.

Returning to England in November 1940, MacNeice ultimately dedicated himself to the war effort, taking a position with the BBC's Features department, which he was offered partly due to family connections. He wrote to Clark explaining that 'the BBC, though deplorable, does leave some loophole for intelligence & individual decisions' and the following month that he did have misgivings about his war work, knowing it was propaganda, 'vulgarisation', but that it had 'its excitements & (what was less to be expected) its value'. It also had its dangers. He gave her his Oxford address to write 'as one never knows how long a London one will last'.

At least now MacNeice felt he had a role. As he told Dodd's wife, 'We play Rummy here every night. It occurs to me that even playing Rummy in London now is a kind of assertion of the Rights of Man, whereas in America it would be nothing but playing Rummy.' Although he informed Eleanor Clark about the possibility of his brief return to America for the BBC, it did not materialise. Their letters continued until MacNeice effectively severed the connection with a brief one in early July 1942, which tells her he has got married to someone, 'but not to anyone I had mentioned to you before'. He hopes they will continue to write 'without post-mortems'. (Clark was to marry Robert Penn Warren in 1952 and to receive the National Book Award for *The Oysters of Locmariaquer* in 1964.)

MacNeice was by no means done with America after that, principally because the country remained vitally important to Britain's war effort. Indeed, to the BBC part of his attraction lay in the fact of his recent experiences and budding reputation there. He had written at length to his father in the summer of 1939 after his first visit that there were a lot of popular misconceptions about America and had enumerated some of them. He had also explored his familiarity with American manners and customs for his readers in *The Strings Are False*, where he celebrated it as a congenial place where people could 'evade the rigours of caste'. And, on his return to England, MacNeice had written five 'London Letters' to the American periodical 'Common Sense', to describe the war on British cities.

In 1941 his first programme for the BBC, 'Word from America', took the form of an anthology of American poems and songs, which was followed by 'Cook's Tour of the London Subways', a fifteen-minute play for an American audience. The following October, MacNeice's play 'Christopher Columbus' was broadcast on the Home Service to mark the 450th anniversary of Columbus's discovery. Also, in 1943, *Meet the US Army* was published, his pamphlet commissioned by the Ministry of Information as a tool for teachers to explain to schoolchildren the culture of our allies.

There were to be later visits to the United States, also. In 1953 MacNeice embarked on another American lecture tour, this time alternating with a recital of song and verse with his wife, the English singer, Hedli Anderson. The following year he returned on a visiting lectureship at Sarah Lawrence College, New York. It is hard to believe that MacNeice might ever have wanted to remain in America. He was not at home there. Then again he was not really at home anywhere. As he had written to his fellow Ulsterman, Dodds, at the war's end, 'I wish one could either <u>live</u> in Ireland or <u>feel oneself</u> in England.' Perhaps it was only in his work that MacNeice was at home. There, time was away and somewhere else.

Old Whaling Days

from *The Personal Narrative of William Barron, Captain.* Hull, 1895

LESLEY HARRISON

1.
about 3 in the afternoon we got fast to a large fish.
after a flourish
she succumbed to us.

2.
the sea began to increase, with showers of snow
as she was hastening towards the
outside of the fiord,

it was with difficulty
they could lash the fins together
and tow her to a place of shelter.

3.
the whale became furious
rolling over and over near us
when she struck the boat,

leaving some of her skin on the sheets.
the harpooner fired a bomb lance
which exploded in a vital part

4.
I saw her under water
she was beautifully distinct, and in slow motion
she lightly touched the vessel.
the concussion made her tremble

5.
one was struck
she led us a nice dance
then went into the pack.

and during the whole time was
perfectly calm, the water smooth

6.
she came to the surface
and two more boats got fast,
leaving three to lance.

and in a few minutes
the sea, the boats and
the men were crimsoned

7.
to shew her rapidity, she immediately
rushed under the floe, down to the bottom

and was hauled up, having
broken her neck,
embedding in the dark blue mud.

8.
she was swimming on her side,
evidently watching our movements.
(but at too great a depth)

From the Archive

Issue 145, May–June 2002

VALERIE DUFF

From a contribution of five poems
alongside 'Akhmatova to her
Husband in Russia' and 'White
Space'. Fellow contributors to this
issue include Marilyn Hacker, John
Gallas, Robert Gray, Moniza Alvi and
Sujata Bhatt.

RUSSIAN CHAPTER

What's fated is the game hen,
the dish of praline dusted in sugar,
servants in rust-red coats,
the big house open for wounded.
An army bottlenecks behind
its horse-backed lieutenants.

Deserters call and wave their sacks
at the carriage bound for Petersburg.
A plump bird in a furry hat,
the young man dreams his unknown wife
he'll meet four years down the road
who now plays cards in Paris.

'Weight of silence' and other poems

GUY GOFFETTE

translated from the French by Marilyn Hacker

Song of Life Passing By

They say that life goes by like a
(*choose one quickly, close your eyes*)
swallow song riverbank or road
where a cyclist rides with astonished breasts

You barely see the candle-wick
diminish and the flame is dead
the goldfish drank the water in
its bowl here's the end's end

(*no more time to choose*) good god
what's a song you never sang
the road in fact you never took
a life when you chose none of it

and when the cyclist has passed by

Emily Dickinson

She's homely, the little cook
but she touches the sky
between the bread-board
and the laundry-basket.

Heavy from loving those roses
far beyond rose-bushes
she flies off with the golden dust
on the furniture.

Inside outside soft where hearts
are stony she rains down
and from the piano sleeping under the sea
draws out a thousand thousand butterflies

that keep the night at bay.

The Date

What is it that's still keeping you here
in the damp air and in the wind
scowling at the lilacs. Is it
the house where in the shadows you once touched

stone bodies and made tears gush forth?
Or the path through the brambles that your steps
let you lose in lassitude
like an old desire, a childhood abandoned

beside the pond, which continues keeping
count of the dead on its own near the sky?
– and you would still like to lean your head
on its frail shoulders before reading

the last date of your days there in the grass.

The Christmas Cashier

Besides her eyes, the scarlet
of her lips, her smile under the whip
of hurried customers, the dreadful syrup
of advertisements and fatigue,

what could I carry more truthful
and more tender toward the star atop
the pine tree, what gift more apt? Nothing
in our hands any longer has weight.

Our dreams are double-parked and from
the shadows' seats in the stalls no Magus
rises any longer but, in
the blind spot, Kaspar the butcher offering

his offal to the steaming snow.

The Weight of Silence

Beginnings abound, but it is always the same story,
about a man the morning grabs by his collar in the street
when he'd gone out to buy a baguette at the bakery.
And there it is, all that he thought was solid in his life, a woman holding a cat among bookshelves
there the street, damp and laughing in first sunlight that smells like a newborn baby,
hurls it all to the ground, the early morning, the sky, the macadam, the bakery,
and all at once he knows nothing
not that he was hungry, not that love exists and stood like the sun in his life, nothing.
A thing like an angel's wing or a bird's has just touched him
and it's as if he stumbled on his shadow, invisible at that hour
and the earth receiving him did not recognize him.

His body is going away alone before his eyes and he watches it without surprise or fright
walk along the city's corridors and lose itself,
with a sort of half-smile, like the smile of the entryway angel whom he no longer remembers.

His weight is exactly the weight of his silence.

After Ronsard

JONATHAN CATHERALL

I.I

Ce premier jour de May, Helene, je vous jure

.I

It's International Workers Day, i.e.
your sense of solidarity means you're unlikely
to fall for anyone invoking eternal nature,
or the way a vine wraps itself round a young elm,
or vegetable love, however biodynamic –
or who goes about in cloth and canvas, pollinating
the world with his green promises. Trust me, I'm not
one of those, and won't, I swear, by no gods
& no masters, on my tattered copy of *Kapital*,
be found doing elsewhat elsewhere with elsewho.
Free love being merely the melting into air,
the laxity in which no revolution sprouts,
a snare of ideology, while the committee
has allotted me and you to leaflet together.

.II

This strip of land no bigger than a thumb
on which I make my choices, pressing down
the carotid artery, the post-industrial
ferment and undergrowth of Spring, the truth-
function's particularly keen sibling
rivalry, and ever those fat nightingales.
In the ninth circle of a bottomless brunch
lie zygote and Zeitgeist, not subject
to chance or the parameters of you.
Blah virtue blah blah, though I hear you
hymned in the eternal mixtape and the
corporate delayering and the strong force
originates in a property known as colour.

.III

You can tell by my pebbledash sculptures & my spiky wood
Nature's stuck up around here
When it's not being torn down or twinned with Bedworth
Or undone by the Laminate Liberation Front &
Dionysus
That's another vine mess you've gotten us into
Will only get so far with the systematic
Deregulation of all the sinsemilla
Remaining as sticky
As a bluebottle's mouthparts
At cross purposes
Je est un autre
Who appears higher up & for longer
In your feed

.IV

springing into seasons
branch & leaf
bank & stream
elliptical
host & parasite
mortal & immortal sexy twins their
kit off in the
stars and other
gnarly binaries
Helen the promises
I promise perform
what they is and
does don't do
get carried away

Exile

I: Origins

ANDRÉ NAFFIS-SAHELY

CIVILISATION BEGETS EXILE; in fact, being banished from one's home lies at the root of our earliest stories, whether human or divine. As the Abrahamic traditions tell us, if disobeying God was our original sin, then exile was our original punishment. In *Genesis*, Adam and Eve are expelled from the Garden of Eden after eating the forbidden fruit, their return forever barred by a flaming sword and a host of Cherubim. Tragedy, of course, repeats itself when Cain murders his brother Abel and is exiled east of Eden. *Genesis* also tells us of The Tower of Babel, an edifice tall enough to reach the heavens itself, a monument to human hubris, whose destruction scattered its people across the earth and 'confounded' our original language, thus making us unintelligible to one another for the first time since creation. The *Tanakh*, in fact, is rife with exile: Abraham sends Hagar and Ibrahim into the wilderness of the Desert of Paran, while the young Moses voluntarily heads into exile after murdering an Egyptian. *Genesis* and *Exodus* tell of the captivity of the Israelites in Egypt and their subsequent escape to Sinai, while the *Book of Ezra* records the end of the Babylonian captivity – the inspiration behind Psalm 137's immortal lines, 'by the rivers of Babylon we sat and wept / when we remembered Zion' – and the eventual return of the Jews to Israel.

Nevertheless, our religious texts tell us that exile wasn't a fate exclusive to lowly humans. In the *Ramayana*, the ancient Indian epic, Rama, the Supreme Being of Hinduism, is banished by his father, the Emperor Dasharatha, after falling victim to court intrigues, and is ordered to spend fourteen years in exile in the forest of Dandaka, seeking enlightenment amidst demons and wandering holy men. Although Rama is recalled from his exile following his father's death, he decides to remain in exile for the entire fourteen years. Similarly, in Greek mythology, Hephaestus, the son of Zeus and Hera, is thrown off Mount Olympus by Hera due to his deformities, only to be brought back to Olympus on the back of a mule by the treacherous God of wine, Dionysus. While exile was often a temporary situation for many gods, it was a more permanent state of affairs for their mortal creations.

It was in Babel's Mesopotamia, towards the end of the Third Dynasty of Ur, that one of our earliest poetic epics, *The Lament for Urim*, first depicted the vicious cycle of conquest and expulsion that has largely characterised our history. In *The Lament for Urim*, Ningal, the goddess of reeds, pleads before the great gods: 'I have been exiled from the city, I can find no rest.' Bemoaning the destruction of her beloved Ur by the invading Elamites, Nigal cries out its name: 'O city, your name exists / but you have been destroyed. / O city, your wall rises high / but your Land has perished.' Employing the refrain 'woe is me', Ningal chronicles the annihilation of her world: 'I am one whose cows have been scattered'; 'My small birds and fowl have flown away'; 'My young men mourn in a desert they do not know'. The Sumerian epic ends with a soft, sanguine prayer that Ningal's city may one day be restored, unleashing one of our first literary archetypes: the hopeful exile. In fact, if *The Lament for Urim* is any indication, the very concept of recorded history – and literature – appears to spring out of the necessity of exile, preserving in our minds what had been bloodily erased on earth.

The ancient Egyptian *Tale of Sinuhe*, written during the Twelfth Dynasty, however, ends on a far happier note. Sinuhe, either a prince or a courtier, depending on the adaptation, flees his native country after an unspecified plot against the throne. Although Sinuhe finds power, wealth and respect in barbaric lands, he cannot quieten the loss that turns all his foreign-won sweetness to ash: 'Desire disturbed me, and longing beckoned my heart. There appeared before my eyes scenes of the Nile and the luxuriant greenery and heavenly blue sky and the mighty pyramids and the lofty obelisks, and I feared that death would overtake me while I was in a land other than Egypt.' Fortunately for Sinuhe, his earnest patriotism wins the Pharaoh's mercy when he returns to Egypt as an old man and he is welcomed back into the fold, able to die in his unforgettable homeland. This uncharacteristically happy conclusion to an exile's suffering shares some similarities with Luke's *Parable of the Prodigal Son*, where the spendthrift younger son returns home to his father's undying love – and to the Biblical tale of Joseph, who is sold into slavery by his envious brothers, but who then rises to unimaginable heights in Egypt, triggering a series of events that would lead to Moses and the Exodus to the Promised Land, the founding myth of the Israelites. As was written in *Exodus*: 'thou shalt not oppress a stranger: for ye know the heart of a stranger, seeing ye were strangers in the land of Egypt.'

While exile has accompanied our every step, and our earliest stories and religious myths are studded with tales of woe and banishment, much has been lost precisely because of exile's oblivion-inducing force. The Greek poet Sappho (c.630–c.570 B C) is perhaps our most famous example. While we know she lived on the island of Lesbos, we do not know what caused her to be exiled to Sicily in her earlier life and only the tiniest fragments of her reputedly voluminous works have survived. Although exile originally appears to have been the outcome of divine retribution, war or intrigue, it wasn't long before humans began to play god with the concept themselves. Greek literature shows us that exile was the most common form of retribution for murder, and exile therefore shapes the stories of many of Greece's most famous mythical heroes, like Peleus, Perseus, Bellerophon or Patroclus, all of whom were killers cast out of society until such time as they could be readmitted. As society grew more complex, however, exile came to be seen as far more useful than simply a punishment for murder. Aristotle's (384–322 B C) *Athe-*

nian Constitution introduces us to the law of ostracism, whereby the names of powerful men suspected of abusing their political offices were submitted to a public vote. Assembling in the agora, citizens would scratch the name of the intended exile onto shards of broken pottery and the shards would be tallied up. The man with the most potshards was subsequently banished. The chosen exile could be sent away permanently or for a period of ten years, at which point they would be welcomed home and their rights duly restored. This practice proved popular enough to spread to the Greek colonies of southern Italy in Magna Graecia. In his *Bibliotheca Historica*, Diodorus Siculus mentions the practice of petalism – from the Greek word for leaf – whereby the citizens of Syracuse wrote the names of the intended exiles on the leaves of olive trees instead of potshards.

Regardless of the voting method, this was the way democracy's enemies were dealt with: if a man grew rich enough to make tyranny inevitable, he was simply banished. Aside from recognising wealth's inherent tendency to subvert the public interest, the particular wisdom of this law lay in its focus on exiling powerful individuals rather than their poorer, more numerous partisans, who were often allowed to remain in the city even when their leaders were not. Exile thus not only offered an attractive alternative to execution, it simultaneously hindered the widening of existing social rifts. Themistocles (c.524–459 B C) was perhaps the most famous of these ostracised exiles. After building the Athenian fleet into a major force and fighting the Persians at Marathon, Artemisium and Salamis, Themistocles was implicated in a plot involving the Spartan tyrant Pausanias – most accounts claim unfairly so – and he was subsequently forced to end his days serving the very Persians he had once warred against.

Almost needless to say, however, war never lagged far behind human lawmaking as the chief wellspring of exile. A fragment by Xenophanes of Colophon (c.570–c.475 B C) provides a clear picture of how the dispersion caused by Greco-Persian Wars fundamentally reshaped Greek society: 'When a stranger appears in wintertime, / these are the questions you must ask, / as you lie reclined on soft couches, / eating nuts, drinking wine by the fire: / 'What's your name?', 'Where do you come from?', / 'How old were you when the Persians invaded?'' Orators, dissidents and artists could be banished just as easily as politicians in ancient Greece, and while many of them were able to secure shelter in faraway cities for some time, exile was never a solid guarantee of safety. Determined to extend his mastery over Greece following his victory in the Lamian War, the Macedonian general Antipater hired a number of 'exile-hunters' to capture anyone who had once defamed or opposed his power. For these exiles, no island was distant enough, no temple imperviously sacred. One of Antipater's most infamous hunters was Archias of Thurii, an actor turned mercenary whose scalps included some of Greece's brightest lights, including Hypereides, Himeraeus, and Demosthenes – who committed suicide by chewing on a poisonous reed after Archias finally tracked him down.

While Greek ostracism was engineered to protect a city's democracy, it was a dictator who first codified exile into Roman law. In 80 BCE, Sulla's *Leges Corneliae* constitutionalized an already established practice: rather than execute convicted criminals, problematic tribunes or ambitious generals, it was deemed easier to expropriate them, thereby enriching the state's coffers, and to banish them from the city. Indeed, Polybius tells us that a Roman citizen accused of a crime could voluntarily go into exile in order to avoid being sentenced. Although banished from the capital, such a citizen could travel to certain *civitates foederatae* – allied cities of Rome – where they could enjoy safety and tranquillity, Neapolis (Naples) being a notable example. As Gordon P. Kelly pointed out in *A History of Exile in the Roman Republic* (Cambridge University Press, 2006), refracted through the prism of Roman law, *exilium* could describe a variety of situations: 'traditional voluntary exile, flight from proscription, magisterial *relegatio*, retirement from Rome for personal reasons, extended military service, and even emigration or travel.' Furthermore, in order to avoid an exile's premature return, the policy of *aquae et ignis interdictio* – exclusion from the communal use of fire and water – created a buffer zone between Rome and the exile's new 'home', making it illegal for anyone to offer said exile a welcome hearth or refreshment within its bounds.

Strictly speaking, however, softer shades of banishment tended to prove the most popular, given that *exilium* technically meant a Roman could be stripped of both his wealth and citizenship, while the lesser *relegatio* ensured said citizen never lost his rights or property. Many of the more famous Roman exiles belonged to the second category. Ovid (43 B C –18 A D), banished to the Black Sea by Augustus, spent much of his time weeping, sighing and penning servile poems which he hoped would restore his good fortunes in the capital, often interrupting his lyricism in mid-flow to remind his readers that he was merely a *relegatus*. As for Cicero (106–43 B C), his letters clearly indicate he spent the majority of his eighteen month exile hopping between luxurious villas, cursing the heavens for his undeserved misfortunes. As such, it is to the stoic Seneca that we must turn for a pragmatic outlook on Roman exile: 'I classify as 'indifferent' – that is, neither good nor evil – sickness, pain, poverty, exile, death. None of these things are intrinsically glorious; but nothing can be glorious apart from them. For it is not poverty that we praise, it is the man whom poverty cannot humble or bend. Nor is it exile that we praise, it is the man who withdraws into exile in the spirit in which he would have sent another into exile.'

Such a sober perspective might have helped Gaius Marius (157–86 BC) make sense of his ironic fate, when after being hounded across Italy by Sulla's wrath, he was turned away by the Roman garrison at Carthage, the very city he had once helped Rome to conquer. Marius would have undoubtedly identified with Shakespeare's Coriolanus: 'Let them pronounce the steep Tarpeian death, / Vagabond exile, flaying, pent to linger / But with a grain a day, I would not buy / Their mercy at the price of one fair word.' Once the Republic perished, Rome's Emperors began to favour the practice of *deportatio insulae*, or deportation to an island. Tiberius, Caligula and Domitian, among others, exiled quite a few of their family members and enemies – not that the two categories were mutually exclusive, especially in Roman society – to the Pontine islands in the Tyrrhenian sea. This exilic tradition in the Tyrrhenian would last for thousands of years – until the end of Benito Mussolini's rule in 1943 – and in its final moments the Pontines housed such prisoners as the novelist Cesare Pavese (1908–1950) and the politician Altiero Spinelli (1907–1986), who wrote his famous pro-European Manifesto while confined to the island of Ventotene.

When Rome slowly began to convert to Christianity, the ensuing ecumenical wars for the empire's soul led to high-ranking clergymen often conspiring to have their rivals exiled, pressuring emperors to intercede on their behalf and stomp out dangerous heresies, thus ensuring the empire's stability. Socrates Scholasticus (c.380–439) relates how, acting under the influence of Bishop Lucius of Alexandria, the Emperor Valens exiled Macarius the Elder and Macarius the Younger to an island off the coast of the Nile inhabited solely by pagans. Disconnected from their communities and fellow worshippers, it was thought the monks would be forced to abandon their faith, a wish that was irremediably dashed when the Macariuses instead converted the island's entire population to the teachings of Christ. While bishops vied with one another and the Constantinian Church acquired a lust for gold and bureaucracy, purging all forms of anti-authoritarian thought from their liturgy, monastic communities sprang up all along the Nitrian Desert, in Lower Egypt, affording the Desert Fathers and Mothers the opportunity to retreat from the increasingly complex, violent and disordered world around them and to devote themselves to God, building upon foundations laid out by earlier mystics such as Saint Anthony of Egypt and Saint Pachomius.

The Egyptian desert – which abounded in what Abba Andrew dubbed the three things most appropriate for a monk 'exile, poverty and endurance in silence' – would also eventually welcome the long-maligned Nestorius. Following his defeat at the Council of Ephesus in 451, when his proposition that Christ's human and divine natures were separate was denounced as irredeemably heretical, Emperor Theodosius II banished Nestorius (c.386–450) to Hibis in Egypt's Western Desert, nevertheless probably ensuring the spread of his teachings to the east, which they did, first via Persia and then on to India and China. Elsewhere, Saint Patrick converted Ireland, alongside Saint Columba, the founder of Iona Abbey, while Saint Aidan established Lindisfarne Priory off the coast of Northumberland. Islands, once home to inconvenient orators and political rivals, became safe-havens for the servants of God, where exile, like in the *Ramayana*, transformed into a form of religious asceticism, a means to purify oneself. Of course, merely withdrawing from the world provided no certainty of instant holiness, as the Desert Father Abba Lucius recognised: 'One day Abba Longinus questioned Abba Lucius about three thoughts saying first, I want to go into exile.' The old man said to him, 'If you cannot control your tongue, you will not be an exile anywhere. Therefore control your tongue here, and you will be an exile.'

Exile

HAWAD

translated from Tuareg, via French, by André Naffis-Sahely

Exile wears away at me, a stalk in a sandstorm
Spells of vertigo, the nausea of withdrawal
a rag waving in the wind
along the tent pegs of desert encampments
The perfume of nostalgia makes me suffocate
like a child carried by the ebb and flow of the waves
The sun shrivels my heart
My eyes are burnt by the look of strangeness
grimaces of ghosts
Worries have carved rivers in my temples
and brow, the marks of life,
like the wrinkles on an old watermelon
along the path of the caravan
which links Ghadamis to Timbuktu
My memories are frozen in the mirages of time
Today, thousands upon thousands of steps to take
alleys of vipers, cliffs of smoky darkness
stand between me and the encampments of long ago
where crows devoured the light of nomadic life
     The ropes of exile are bound with a sailor's knot
     Anguish hones me into a needle of pain
     Years after years have gone by
I'm a trace remnant of my dreams
So many nights have flowed past me
I dance inside the flames

I have tasted the syrups of countless fruits
the perfumes of innumerable flowers,
mint, jasmine, pomegranate,
the freshness of gardens
filled with palm trees, the shade of palaces
mosques of the distant East.

I have listened to the echo of tears
the bastardization of all agreements
I have rocked myself in the swing-chairs of dawn

Yet nothing soothed my howling.
     I said
where are the tents of long ago
impregnated with the indigo of the ahal ceremonies?
Where are the tents of times gone by
their entrances aligned with the horizon of the stars
the desert of border-free roaming?
Where have the seasons of swapping pastures gone
Lessons on love and beauty? Where are the plains of mirage
where young camels
and gazelles graze
watched over by boys
wearing braided belts
     To this day, I can hear the joyous cries
of brave warriors

I still see the silhouettes of antelopes
with elongated necks in the setting sun
the mistresses of the ahal ceremonies
The smile of the moon
       Kha! Fingers gently caressing
the violin of honor
which takes us to the rooftop of constellations
beyond time
       Khay! There's no remedy for my burns
because my dreams have been swept away
by the dragon-machines
and their whirlwinds of steel

pinned under the paws of hyenas
       How wrong I was to trust the rudder
of the ship of life to scarecrows
who led the vessel adrift in the storm
       We will carry the spark of this exile
to the throne-room of galaxies
to the kingdoms of sparks that plunge
into the oceans of light
Because the pain of our exile will blend
with the wailing of the traveler's
soul

Poems from 'God of Corn'

DAVID TROUPES

Each poem begins with a title or passage from Josiah Gilbert Holland's 1855 book, *A History of Western Massachusetts*.

The Weather Was Extremely Cold

Enough now for a month. And the sun has gone down.
I suppose there's something of the sun
in the wood stacks, and
of June, and our new boy.
I suppose this winter forest
is thrown like a shadow. But I do feel
when the sun goes down
there is a moment, like a quick holler
and no echo,
when time stops, lifts away, if you understand.
And I can set down my ax
and raise my hands a little,
say each six inches from my side, and there is light
despite the sun having gone,
and my arms float free of the weight of my shirt,
and my feet
find the comfortable centers
of my boots. The wind no longer arrives, it is a cold
breathing of the earth.
The moon has fastened to its stump.
If I find the crow the crow
is found. If a branch falls
it is a scepter
taken up.
The great stone is only just split. And the hunters
will never return, they are lost to the hills, a last portage
of hope.
It is only with my feet that I touch the earth –
a slight cross,
chance flower. There is something
here
lighting such lamps as I can follow.

That Part of Northfield Known as 'Grass Hill'

Humid gourds. August darkness. By the hill
jays
slip and sew.
Girls are picking bilberries
for their smock-pockets. They bow
tangled – jam for the closet and
a bone meal moon.
Months then – and two
will die –
before March
and the haberdashery of spring, the rag and soap
of willow.
Older brothers darken to their work, the earth
is blacked and greened
and the girls for their games
break
apart in a plasma of wildflower.

A Narrow Valley

A narrow valley runs the whole length of the town, from Stafford to Palmer on the North, diversified by rich meadow, ridges of sand, and small boulders. The New London, Willimantic and Palmer Railroad passes through this valley. East and West of this are hills, running North and South, which possess productive soil, suitable for grazing and tillage.

One day a few years ago a train – and from here
you can just see the line – stopped,
broken down.
Bulbs of steam and smoke. After a time
folk came out, little seeds
of color to my bad eyes.
They were not expecting this – miles
from a platform, and how strange to be
in the unknown middle
of two known ends.
Today
I have seen two trains
and neither stopped. It's late September
and a haze holds
warmly over the brown harvest-hack,
the many graves of August. The air
is a second land

with its tables and ponds.
This slight hill gives a slight
heaven, a parity
with the busy crows and the willow-fire. Whitely
the earth
diminishes into sun. The farm shines
like what I know of the sea
and I see my wife has hung our bed linen
on the porch line for the wind, a waterless
scouring
by which the sheets are made cold and we lie at night
in that cold, that air
of washed linen, and by our bodies make it warm.
The tools I had put down I take up.
There is work to be done
on the fence
at the farthest corner.

Thom Gunn

The Young Existentialist Conqueror

M. C. CASELEY

I

IN HIS ESSAY 'Cambridge in the Fifties',[1] Thom Gunn wrote autobiographically about his time as an undergraduate. He self-deprecatingly presented both his Forsterian illusions about the place and gave valuable glimpses of his early encounters with the likes of Karl Miller and Ted Hughes. Very early poems such as 'The Secret Sharer' appeared whilst he was still a student there, and his essay in fact locates the setting for this piece precisely, at the corner of Jesus Lane and Sidney Street. Already, in this poem, typical Gunn ideas of doubleness allied to a slightly outmoded Elizabethan diction ('O') appear, and although Gunn himself later tended to underplay the poems eventually published in *Fighting Terms* in 1954, their energy and youthful ambition are still impressive. Important early exercises such as 'Carnal Knowledge' and 'Tamer and Hawk' evince a tough sense of balance and form whilst withdrawing, at times, from indulgent, overt displays of emotion.

In another of the *Occasions of Poetry* essays, 'My Life up to Now', Gunn outlined his debt to Donne and Shakespeare, describing his poetry of the time as 'the act of an existentialist conqueror, excited and aggressive',[2] and the sexual negotiations in 'The Wound' and 'Lofty in the Palais de Danse' certainly fit this description. The swaggering boasting of Lofty, in the latter, makes it a divisive poem to teach to a mixed-sex group of sixth-formers: Gunn's distancing irony must be carefully explored if any sympathy at all is to be extended to him. However, there is finely-judged ambiguity and even the 'rhetorical awkwardness'[3] Gunn accused himself of cannot disguise the success of many of these poems, as they introduce typical Gunn protagonists, questing anti-heroes who recur in his subsequent, more famous second volume, *The Sense of Movement* (Faber 1957).

Teaching these poems to sixth-formers over the past decade has allowed me to appreciate them anew. I had always admired the later, free verse Gunn, especially *The Man with Night Sweats*, but now I learned to appreciate the diamond-hard toughness of the earlier verse, and see how the two stages were connected. It was evident that these early poems were not just museum pieces. My students, reading Angry Young Men like Alan Sillitoe and John Osborne, also picked up on Gunn's eye for a prophetic phrase and his ability to inhabit popular culture

---

1 To be found in *The Occasions of Poetry* (Faber and Faber, 1982, edited by Clive Wilmer).

2 p. 183, Gunn, op. cit.
3 p.184, Gunn, op. cit.

in a way that contemporaries such as Larkin and Hughes could not: to put it another way, Larkin may have been an aficionado of trad. jazz, but Gunn wore a leather jacket and instinctively understood Elvis, rock'n'roll and James Dean.

II

My own interest in Gunn's poetry made teaching it a pleasure and it was also refreshing to think that students were being exposed to someone other than the ubiquitous Heaney or Larkin. Gunn was someone who could give them radically different perspectives on the 1950s (and the 1960s and 1970s, if they explored his later work – there were always one or two who discovered the later Gunn and returned with questions). Nevertheless, I was dumbfounded one day to pick up, cheaply in a Lincolnshire secondhand bookshop, a handsome Nonesuch Press edition of Milton inscribed: 'Thom Gunn, Trinity College, Cambridge, Oct 1950'. I went home clutching my serendipitous find and checked the dates in the essays: yes, Gunn went to Trinity in 1950, after his National Service, yes, he writes of Leavis lecturing there, so, yes, this could be his copy.

It was even more exciting and interesting to find that large sections of 'Paradise Lost' had been heavily annotated in pencil, and the handwriting seemed to match Gunn's name in the flyleaf; several of these comments quote C.S. Lewis approvingly. What did Gunn take from his study of Milton? The essays in *The Occasions of Poetry* do not enlighten us. Interestingly, however, when he comes to discuss questions of hierarchy in *Paradise Lost*, Lewis describes attitudes Gunn might endorse: 'tyranny... is rebellion', he says and, later, describes how 'discipline' allows a virtuous freedom: it 'exists for the sake of what seems its very opposite... the pattern deep hidden in the dance... alone gives freedom to the free, wild gestures that fill it'.[4] Consider alongside this, Gunn's discussion of Basil Bunting's poetry:[5] after quoting a passage from *Briggflatts*, he calls it 'an old dream of order... the hierarchy of shepherds over sheepdogs, of sheepdogs over sheep.'

Other annotations are brief insights, gleaned in the lecture hall perhaps: Milton's style is descibed in Lewis's words as 'magnanimous austerity', an intriguing paradox, whilst a marginal comment at the end of Book IV notes that 'there is no doubt that Satan gets the better of this encounter'. The waking of Eve at the beginning of the next book elicits this judgement: 'this might almost be called Chaucerian in its simplicity' whilst the later fruit-tasting is described as 'Cordon Bleu'! Gunn's appreciation of Milton is also evident at the end of Book V: the passages beginning 'O argument blasphemous' is praised as 'superbly controlled verse of amazing power and persuasion'. At this point, fascinating though they are, it is worth pointing out that many of these pencil comments are very faint, and some seem to be in a different hand: those I am quoting are the ones which I am pretty certain

are written in the same handwriting style as the ownership name cited above.

In Book VI, Grierson is quoted approvingly alongside Abdiel's response to Satan: 'this argument is the central theme of P Lost and of all that Milton wrote – the supremacy of reason, the identification of true freedom with obedience to reason or conscience'. Gunn pursues this theme later, in Book VIII: 'Reason again named superior – physical love, though pleasing and essential is not true love – But human, rational things – a spiritual love the highest'. This later manifests itself in poems demonstrating what Gunn called his 'theory of pose': in 'Carnal Knowledge', for example, the narrator comments that 'an acute girl would suspect / my thoughts might not be, like my body, bare'.[6]

This rationalising distance is everywhere in these early poems, and a further Gunn theme recurs against the comment 'our reason is our law' (Book IX): 'Free will'. A few pages later, alongside Book X, comes this: 'free will is man's greatest faculty, by which he can gain redemption or damnation'. *Fighting Terms*, which appeared in 1954, is full of characters exercising their free will, often to the detriment of the relationships they negotiate. This can particularly be seen in 'Carnal Knowledge' and 'Lofty in the Palais de Danse'. The protagonists in these two poems – and they are *dramas* of seduction – explore the emotions of seduction and sex, but always there is an awareness of free will, of choices deliberately taken: 'You are not random picked', says Lofty to an unnamed girl plucked from a dancefloor, while 'I am not what I seem', boasts the poseur in the former poem. Always their choices are mediated by reason and acts of the will; Lofty becomes truly a fallen Satan: 'Like the world, I've gone to bad' he boasts with weary complacency.[7]

Are these early anti-heroes truly Byronic fallen angels, then? Gunn roughs out his 'theory of pose' in the early essay quoted above: a heady cocktail of Donne, Yeats, Stendhal and Sartre. The role-playing extended into his own life: 'viewing myself as an actor trying to play a part provided rich material for poetry', he states.[8] Gunn's questing heroes, following their impulses of the will, are national servicemen, a role he himself had played: both Lofty and the neo-Achilles of 'The Wound' can fit this clothing. 'Incident on a Journey', the final poem, picks up some of these ideas again: a red-coated soldier spectrally visits a deserter – or a questing anti-hero – but delivers no warning to be heeded. Instead, the shifting refrain is a boast that he regrets nothing. Having died in 'a minute far beyond a minute's length', as a result of acting on a 'living impulse', he rises 'will-less'.[9] The first-person narrator resolves to be like him; he, too, will respond to his impulses and regret nothing. It is revealing to contrast these figures with the long note written at the end of Book XII of *Paradise Lost*: 'N.B. Satan has

4   *A Preface to Paradise Lost*, C.S.Lewis (Oxford University Press, 1942), pp. 78, 81.
5   *The Occasions of Poetry*, p. 157.

6   'Carnal Knowledge', lines 3–4, *Fighting Terms*, Thom Gunn (Fantasy Press, 1954, Faber, 1962).
7   'Lofty in the Palais de Danse', lines 1, 11, 'Carnal Knowledge', line 7, both in *Fighting Terms*, Gunn.
8   'Cambridge in the Fifties', in *The Occasions of Poetry*.
9   Lines 23, 18, 28 respectively, 'Incident on a Journey', in *Fighting Terms*.

faded away. His doom is foretold certainly, and then he matters no more and <u>Man</u> has the final scene as they leave Paradise, possessing above all Hope, and God's promise of redemption. How, therefore, can Satan possibly be the hero?! <u>Man</u> in weakness and humility is the hero – human nature, perhaps the seat of the divine possibilities controlled by Reason and free will. The poem ends on a note of infinite hope.'

One minor poem in *Fighting Terms* might suggest, however, that Gunn continued to explore these specific ideas of being cast out of the bliss of paradise. In 'Looking Glass', the controlling metaphor of the poem is a garden, specifically named Eden, but it is charmed, trapped within a looking-glass. The first-person narrator, a cast-out Adam, characterises himself as 'the gardener' and though there are Miltonic echoes, the theology is blurred: 'It was not innocence lost, not innocence / but a fine callous fickleness […] gratification being all'. A later revision loosened the vision of Edenic decay still further, from 'my green towers sweetly go to seed', to

an approving, 'It goes to seed. How well it goes to seed.'[10] Here, too, the speaker is a typical Gunn existential wanderer, homeless and, like Lofty, cast out from bliss, aware of his own unworthiness: the poem ends with a sudden description of his movements, 'from town to town, damp-booted, unemployed'.[11] Another parallel could be the divisions of 'The Secret Sharer', a doppelgänger poem, as the speaker, as well as being cast out, sees himself framed inside the glass: enjoyment, pleasure and gratification all tantalisingly available. This is the 'box of tricks' Gunn himself would celebrate in his later work, although by this time, he had long moved away from these youthful dramas of reason and energy, as circumstances in San Francisco turned him into the celebrated elegist of *The Man with Night Sweats*.

10 This revision can be found in Gunn's *Collected Poems* (Faber, 1993), p. 22.
11 Lines 13, 8–11, 30, 'Looking Glass', in *Fighting Terms*.

Mother as Spy

PATRICK MCGUINNESS

Mother as Widow

The barely-perceptible drag
of the marriage she's carrying:
like a bird who's been tagged
and who flies with the weight
of its near-weightless ring.

Mother as Spy

All of our words for spying are taken
from the dictionary of sleep;
though it is the spy who is awake,
and the world around her sleeps.

This is my life, she thinks, *I am in deep cover,*
embedded in my motherhood, my marriage,
the things they see but which I'm something other
than. We eat and sleep and breathe and age

together – he and I; me and him;
the neighbours and me with our smiles.
I wait in lines. I taxi the children
from accomplishment to small

accomplishment. I cheer on touchlines.
I watch their hidden teenage lives
make smoke in the mirror as I drive.
They think because they're new to lies

it means I must be too. They cultivate
their own things which they learn to hide.
At first it's hard, because lying is to push a large thing
through a small hole in the language.

I am always waiting for the call.
When it comes, will I recognise the voice?
Was there a password?
I think my handler may have died;

been purged.

Squeeze the Day

is how I heard the line the first time around:
Carpe diem. 'Squeeze the day!' I told them proudly;

The language of juicing seemed right for Horace,
and though my version amounted to more or less

the same, it had a better ring,
more urgent, and *squeeze* was closer

to what I wanted but didn't have the words for;
or what my body wanted, at school, at home,

and my body had not yet spoken to my mind:
because squeezing was to seize and to be seized

in return, to have the day seize you.
But when I learned what Horace really said,

when at last the day was there for squeezing,
it was dry.

Poetry

In *Singing in the Rain*, Debbie Reynolds plays a woman with a good voice who replaces the beautiful silent screen star Lina Lamont, who is grating and vulgar and is about to be vocally unmasked by the arrival of sound. The elocution lessons don't work and she can't lip-sync; you can't teach class, the film tells us, and class is authenticity.

Later I found out that Jean Hagen, the actor playing Lina Lamont, had the good voice, the better voice, and it was her voice they used when Debbie Reynolds pretended it was her voice pretending to be Lina's. The voice had been dubbed back to source.

I was never sure what there was to learn there, but now it strikes me as a pretty good definition of poetry. You start out silent, then borrow another voice and try to fit it to your mouth. It doesn't work. You keep trying until finally – yes! – you have it: your own voice. But now it's the mouth that's no longer yours.

Naming the Animals

First, just the one word: not doing as he asked,
not coming when he called; like a dog, like the word
dog, disobedient, sullenly joining the pack-hounds,
the uncollared, past the perimeter and out of town.

Others followed, until he no longer knew
if it was he or they who left.
If he needed the word now he designed
all he had to say around its absence.

It started at table, with *venison*.
It always had something of the forest to it:
musky, rustling, its sound so far, as meat
in the mouth, from the *deer* it lived as
that one day he knew the word
only from the shadow that it cast
in heartbeats, hiding in some doubtful thicket
where his tongue no longer goes.

Then all the animals.

One by one they left, became a forest at night,
a sea in the dark, the species coming loose from their names,
throwing them off like saddles. Horses bucking the word *horse*.
The dog biting the word that said it.

'That bit', he says – we are all listening now,
his conversation has become a room everyone drifts into,
nods at everyone else, then leaves again, a party
you need to show your face at and then go –

'that bit in the Bible:
And whatsoever Adam called every living creature,
that was the name thereof...
it's what's happening to me backwards'.

Prose Between Stations

for Micky Sheringham

Things seen/heard from the top floor of the Brussels/Luxembourg Inter-City Express (only the train is fast – life inside and out takes place in some other zone of time, as thickly weightless as footage of an astronaut cooking breakfast between planets):

At Ciney a bull nonchalantly mounting a cow (this is outside the train)
as the cow grazes on, pestling mouthfuls of grass with a slow swing of her jaw. She chews in time to his slack thrusts, each one hovering effortfully at the edges of itself, as if pulling into and out of velcro. This is the middle-distance, with neither the prestige of the faraway nor the imperiousness of foreground. The whole scene depends on the train's speed, which allows the traveller, forehead laid refreshingly against the glass, to pick it out with a distinctness and granularity that is at first disproportionate to its interest, but which quickly becomes its interest.

At Ottignies, students from Louvain-la-Neuve climb aboard with backpacks full of laundry for their mothers to wash: a journey of twenty minutes undertaken with a month of clothing. They are equipped to emigrate, but instead descend, as they always do, twenty minutes later, at Gembloux,
where

three workmen off the day shift at a zinc-plating factory step on and talk about their friend who hanged himself yesterday, the evening of the burial of his wife, dead last month of a pulmonary thrombosis. At Namur

three kindergarten teachers replace them seat for seat, discuss the school's Christmas decorations, affectionately mention a troublesome boy they like but whose life is in danger of going... (one of them searches for the right phrase, then with a little laugh gestures around her and says with a sort of embarrassed satisfaction:) *off the rails*, then settle down to comparing different brands of sleeping tablet with the discrimination and adjectival range of sommeliers discussing vintages.

The sky is a mild, uninsistent grey, streaked with oily-looking damp like those little cloths they put on headrests of armchairs in old people's homes.

This raw material thinks of all the contortions it would have to go through to become a poem, and decides to stay as it is: nondescript, if not undescribed.

'Secant Lads' and other poems

DANIEL KING

Secant Lads

You are monads, loved for a moment
Attached to me as acolytes
Chords but not diameters, bowmen
Who chant my mantra, solstice nights:

Secant lads, secant lads, secant lads, secant lads
Secant lads, secant lads, secant lads, secant lads
Secant lads, secant lads, secant lads, secant lads

You are nomads, castle encircling
As venomous as aconite;
Tiger moths from Saturn, checkmating
With darts or arrows, sound or light;

You are comrades, Diaz in daring,
As dear to me as ammonites;
Sand from Sagittarius, blasting
With chords of Ø, you topaz knights!

Butterflies

Satellites with solar wings
Titanium butterflies that drift
Larva free around the moon
In black and white eclipsing rings
Flee lycaenid Earthlight rays
To hover bright and perilune
Brittle steel antennae primed
To sip on signals from our shift.

Lava tubes are what we gift
Our regolith descents are timed
Days ahead for early noon
At sunrise Sulawesi's K
Greets our climb and how we sing
Our news as bright as rubies strewn
Filter free, for Earth will lift
Its people crowned like rutile kings.

Tyr Metaphysics

Chrome skinned ancient foes with the night
In their hair
Will see arrowing in their path
Tyr's T rune transformed for Kalki
And his Delta K primed
With a stare.

Sea born Tor, he curbs with his arms;
He is heir
And we, worshipping with this hymn,
Raise high hard titanium stipes
With the Tuesday broadheads
If we dare.

Blue eyes probe our minds and we feel
As if air
A gale spiraling with the force
Weak souls crushed and made to obey
We submit our life's will
With our prayer.

Googling Prynne

The Oval Window: A New Annotated Edition, J. H. Prynne
eds. N. H. Reeve and Richard Kerridge (Bloodaxe) £12

THE NEW BLOODAXE EDITION of *The Oval Window* by J.H. Prynne is an illustrated, annotated reprint. The first edition ('Cambridge, 1983') was privately printed for the poet in Saffron Walden and distributed by Duck Soup, a bookshop run by Nick Kimberley, veteran of the celebrated counter-culture institutions, Compendium and Indica, and editor in the late sixties of *Big Venus*, a short-lived magazine which printed Andrew Crozier, Allen Fisher and Lee Harwood, alongside Ashbery and other Americans. The covers of the 1983 edition unfold into a photograph of a stone wall with 'a rough opening', whited out to frame the only text:

'THE OVAL WINDOW / *J. H. Prynne*'.

A parallelogram with concavities at right and left, its shape, as Ian Patterson pointed out years ago, isn't even approximately oval.

It is not the only puzzling opening, as Richard Kerridge acknowledges: 'If we are looking for conventional linear sense, the opening lines are disconcerting' – perhaps an understatement:

The shut inch lively as pin grafting
leads back to the gift shop, at a loss

for two-ply particles

set callow,
set bland and clean, wailing as when

to wait is block for scatter.

Two obscure entities are compared; one 'leads' us, if only 'back', then leaves us 'at a loss' – after two lines. Who or what is 'wailing'? How helpful is the implied elucidation, 'as when'? In what context could the indented phrase, 'set callow', even make sense? Google cites *Child Study* (1950): '[Counsel] not as one who would set callow youth on the right path, but as a fellow thinker'; and Daniel Defoe on 'Old Jacobites', 'who having lost their Estates at Play, turn Sharpers, and make it their Business to set Callow Heirs' – but we're none the wiser.

For once. To introduce Google is Kerridge's own first move. A 'transformative development' of 'the practice of reading', now to be conducted, as an option, 'with search engine at hand', it gives access, for example, to precise horticultural usage of the phrase 'pin grafting', which might identify the 'shut inch' as 'the pin-shaped scion inserted in the grafting operation'. And time and again, in reading Prynne, Google comes up with the goods. I still recall the shock of delight at identifying the infernal 'angelic sub-/strate' in 'Of Sanguine Fire' as 'luciferin'. For all that, however, Kerridge's aptest comment on the opening owes nothing to Google at all: 'A gift shop... at any leisure-site of potentially ambitious cultural... interest... embodies the... commodification of the attraction, and an effortless, reductive form of consumption... [T]here is a comic challenge to the reader in the idea of someone giving up after a few minutes, turning back and settling for the gift shop.'

This elegant interpretation of 'back to the gift shop, at a loss', had never occurred to me, nor, apparently, until now, to Kerridge, whose joint exploration of this poem with N.H. Reeve has been one of the most illuminating critical enterprises of the last thirty-odd years – for them, no doubt, but I meant for the rest of us. It makes a convincing link with their earlier themes: '[T]he recurrent image... of the toy snowstorm... a typical piece of gift shop merchandise... has a teasing resemblance to two [others]: the stone shelter, a small redoubt temporarily holding together in a swirling world, and the Oval Window in the inner ear, with its flakes, the otolith crystals, shifting... with the body's movement so as to stabilise the individual's orientation and sensory intake.'

When *Nearly Too Much*, the first book-length study of Prynne, appeared from Liverpool University Press in 1995, Reeve and Kerridge had already been writing about his poetry for ten years. I first came across their work in 1985, when an early response to *The Oval Window* appeared in *The Many Review*, and I note that it makes no reference to the otolith crystals, which are at the heart of the expanded interpretation in Drew Milne's *Parataxis* in 1993. The further expansion into the final chapter of *Nearly Too Much* runs to over forty pages, whilst the reprint of the *Parataxis* piece in John Tranter's online magazine *Jacket* (No. 20, 2002) has illustrations of the otolith crystals and a diagram of the inner ear.

This 'New Annotated Edition' is in five parts, symmetrically arranged: an essay by Kerridge; a clean text of the poem; sixteen photographs, including the one cropped for the cover, and a diagram; the annotated text; and an essay by Reeve. Instead of covering any or all names, quotations and terminology that might be unfamiliar, annotation is limited, with very few exceptions, to previously unrecorded sources from a composition archive made over by Prynne, including the photographs and diagram (all of the same Cumbrian shieling), clippings from the *Financial Times*, a manual entitled *Elements of Computer Programming* and an anthology of Chinese poetry. Revelations, and no mistake – but by the terms of reference the phrase 'lightly clad' incurs an attribution to a *Times* review of ZZ Top at 'Monsters of Rock' in 1983, yet 'like a bird on the wing' escapes scot-free, despite the relevance of the Skye Boat song to the immediate context of Highland clearances and test-drilling for oil. *Jacket*-style illustrations of the beautiful 'found' poetry of physiology would have added a dimension, if space could not have been found for the editors' classic account of 'the organ through which gravity speaks'. Admittedly, any such deficit can be made good by reading *Nearly Too Much*.

As to the new material, what is on offer, if anything, that might prompt an update of the immersive, pre-Google engagement in the book? Take #19, in the annotated version:

Her wrists shine white like the frosted snow;[1]
they call each other to the south stream.[2]

The oval window is closed in life,
by the foot-piece of the stapes.[3] **Chill shadows**
fall from the topmost eaves,[4] **clear waters**
run beside the blossoming peach.[5] **Inside**
this window is the perilymph of the vestibule.[3]
　　Now O now I needs must part,
　　parting though I absent mourne.[6]
It is a child's toy, shaken back in
myopic eddies **by the slanting bridge:**[7]
toxic; dangerous fire risk; **bright moonlight**
floods the steps like a cascade of water.[4]

The first two lines are amongst four quotations which, according to the authors in 1995, 'very much resemble English renderings of the "Palace Style Poetries" of the Southern Dynasties, which Prynne discussed with considerable erudition in a critical essay appended to Anne Birrell's translation of the anthology *New Songs from a Jade Terrace*'. Now, however, we learn that, besides the quotation from John Dowland, there are on this single page six discontinuous exact quotations, dating, not from the Southern Dynasties, but from the Later Shu dynasty, all from *Among the Flowers*, an anthology compiled by Chao Ch'ung-tso in the mid-tenth century; and that, from #18 to #26, there are a total of thirty, with an occasional ellipsis or alteration, from lyrics by Wei Chuang (836–910) and Sun Kuang-hsien (898–968), cited in #19, and six other poets. An equivalent fast-forward would take us from Chaucer to Blake. We also learn that they are restricted to the final third of the poem – earlier tropes in a similar vein, such as 'the moon is bright as snowy day' (#14), attract no annotation.

This is the more intriguing in view of an antithetical series, restricted to sections #1–#15, to which attention is drawn by one of the few notes to a single word (#2): 'rabbit': London cab-drivers' slang for gossip, the latest stories, rumours, etc.' It took the hint from Prynne himself to impart a cockney accent to a series of locutions such as 'a proper tonic'; 'cut up rough'; 'have a heart'; 'talk of the town'; 'keep mum'; 'precious little'; 'flat out'; 'on the nail'; 'do keep up'; etc. Then, from #16 on, the inflection fails to fit a single phrase. The contrast is pointed by a disconcerting overlap, an ironic cliché (#1): 'Ah so' is defined by the OED as, 'Exclamation. humorous, derogatory; used in representations or imitations of Japanese or, by misidentification, Chinese speech'. Following Kerridge, the travesty of the polite Japanese acknowledgement, *'ah so* desu ka', might be interpreted as another 'comic challenge', imputing guilt by association, and by contrast, to yet another series of tropes, this time fully annotated, from the supposedly more dignified London of political and financial power (#3):

　　Safe in our hands,[1]
won't cut up rough, at all, pent up
and boil over.

　　1. *The Times*, 22 August 1983: 'Several local health authorities are now treating with scepticism the Prime Minister's statement during the election campaign that the service "is safe in our hands"'.

At the risk of stereotyping 'London cabdrivers', it would be hard to improve on the epitome of Thatcher's speeches as 'rabbit by proxy'. The point is not that anyone would have missed the topical irony of such phrases as '**Being asked to cut / into the bone**[1]', but that, thanks to the 'proxy' dig in the ribs, we might awake to another dimension of this inexhaustible poem.

Reeve and Kerridge are wide awake to its apocalyptic dimension, using the adjective three times each in a combined total of forty pages of superb new commentary on topics that range from the myth of Erysichthon to the Blue Streak silo near Tinkler Crags. Look, for example, at the physiological detail about the closure of the oval window 'in life', with the poignant implication, sustained in the idea of 'parting' at the 'vestibule', that it might open in death. It is 'fitting to be known' that the words 'in life' occur in the (wonderful) source text, *Anatomy, Regional and Applied* by R.J. Last, meaning, perhaps, not only in the dissected cadaver. Last supplies a stream of scientific poeticisms and, in comparing the 'cochlear canal' to 'the spiral slide at a fun fair', may even have suggested the metaphor of the 'child's toy'. Interrelations between deaths and entrances, physiological, architectural and metaphysical, are noted throughout this edition, as in *Nearly Too Much*. If, after referral of the phrase 'in a twinkling' (#1) to its Pauline source (1 Corinthians 15:52: 'in the twinkling of an eye, at the last trump'), the Apocalyptic dimension receives short shrift, it is primarily due to the different emphases in the documentation vouchsafed by Prynne. Take these beautiful lines from #26:

> In **darkness by day**[1] we must press on,
> Giddy at the tilt of **a negative crystal**.[2]

The first note cites 'The Nine Songs' of an ancient Chinese shaman, translated by Arthur Waley: 'All is murk and gloom. Ch'iang! Darkness by day! / The east wind blows gust on gust, spreading magic rain'; the second a definition of 'birefringence' in 'a negative crystal' from *Concepts of Classical Optics* (1958), a property discovered in calcite crystals such as the otoliths in the inner ear. It would only supplement this invaluable data to invoke the darkness at the break of noon in Luke's gospel (23:44–45): 'And it was about the sixth hour, and there was a darkness over all the earth until the ninth hour. And the sun was darkened, and the veil of the temple was rent in the midst' (*kalypsis* being Greek for 'veil'); and the source of the vision of St John the Divine in the prophet Ezekiel (1:22): 'And the likeness of the firmament upon the heads of the living creature was as the colour of the terrible crystal'.

Again, much in the completely unannotated final section, #27, has already been discussed, including the concept of 'herbage', in the context of transhumance by Cumbrian families, who would occupy an upland shieling, such as the one extensively documented by Prynne, between May and Lammastide in August; the cosmic connotations of 'plasma'; and the 'child's toy' in the last line from the 'gift shop' in line two, emblematic of how, 'in a twinkling', 'we shall be changed' (same verse of Corinthians); and of how we sustain, or lose, our moral and physiological equilibrium as the otolith crystals swirl. It

is a fine point, well taken, that the astonishing conclusion might be relieved of bold text and superscripts:

> Free
> to leave at either side, at the fold line
> found in threats like herbage, the watch
> is fearful and promised before. The years
> jostle and burn up as a trust plasma.
> Beyond help it is joy at death itself:
> a toy hard to bear, laughing all night.

Yet a cluster of texts might be adduced to illuminate the spontaneous combustion of time. Like a transhumant community in search of optimum 'herbage' for their 'fold', or 'at the fold line' in a landscape of stratified rock, the 'shepherds abiding in the field', 'keeping watch' and 'sore afraid', are reassured in Luke's gospel by 'tidings of great joy' (2:8–10); whilst the words 'promised before', salient yet awkward in context, refer in one of St Paul's epistles to the 'hope of eternal life, which God, that cannot lie, promised before the world began' (Titus 1:2). The Apocalyptic guarantee that 'there should be time no longer' (Revelation 10:6) might account for 'joy at death itself', expressed in strikingly similar terms by John Donne in the 'Seventh Meditation' of *Devotions Upon Emergent Occasions* (1624): 'Men have died of joy, and almost forbidden their friends to weep for them, when they have seen them die laughing' (with a glance at the 'Seventh Prayer': 'thou hast let me see in how few hours thou canst throw me beyond the help of man'). In the same key as Prynne's expostulations upon (im)mortality, Donne's hyperbole gives a hysterical edge to the proverbial laughter of Democritus, whilst resolving the anguished doubts of his 'First Meditation': 'God, who as he is immortal himself, had put a coal, a beam of immortality into us, which we might have blown into a flame, but we blew it out, by our first sin... we cannot enjoy death, because we die in this torment of sickness... Is this the honour which man hath by being a little world, that he hath these earthquakes in himself, sudden shakings, these lightnings, sudden flashes...?'

Like Prynne, Donne is raiding a textbook on anatomy, *Microcosmographia: A Description of the Body of Man* by Helkiah Crooke, whose title highlights the parallel between the 'little world' of the body, the 'toy snowstorm' and the temporal macrocosm 'blown into a flame'. An account of the vitalist phenomenology of the 'solid and fluid world of flesh and blood', common to all three poets, is to be found in Dylan Thomas's 'Defence of Poesie' (1933):

> The greatest description... of our own 'earthiness' is... in John Donne's *Devotions*, where he describes man as earth of the earth, his body earth, his hair a wild shrub growing out of the land. All thoughts and actions emanate from the body. Therefore the description of a thought or action – however abstruse it may be – can be beaten home by bringing it on to a physical level. Every idea, intuitive or intellectual, can be imaged... in terms of the... flesh, skin, blood, sinews, glands, organs, cells, or senses.

Thomas lifted his title, *Deaths and Entrances*, from Donne's sermons, and John Goodby has traced the elusive 'Death's feather' to its source in the 'Seventh Meditation': 'There is scarce anything that hath not killed somebody; a hair, a feather hath done it'. Donne's 'Third Expostulation', which finds him languishing 'in the door of the grave', inspires the climax of *Under Milk Wood*: 'Knock twice, Jack, / At the door of my grave / And ask for Rosie'. The 'oval window' itself is one of Blake's 'doors of perception', the 'points of inlet and outlet' at the 'frontiers of physical human identity' noted by Reeve and Kerridge in *Nearly Too Much*, its allegorical significance given a twist in the closing and opening lines of sections #20–21:

all day long, the red door is closed.

So: from now on too, or soon lost,
the voice you hear is your own...

The note cites a lyric by Mao Hsi chen (fl. 940), but the parallel with the closure 'in life' of the oval window carries across into the quotation, retrieved by Google, from an apocalyptic American bestseller of the second world war, *Generation of Vipers* by Philip Wylie (1942): 'Whenever the door of Hell opens, the voice you hear is your own.'

As elucidated and now annotated and considered afresh by Reeve and Kerridge, *The Oval Window* is a landmark not only of Prynne's poetry, but also of his philosophy. It stands between two strange, enthralling texts, the 1963 essay, 'Resistance and Difficulty', and the 2011 prose-poem, with long quotations and a page of 'Reference cues' to Aristotle, Boethius, Langland and Shelley, *Kazoo Dreamboats; or, On What There Is*. 'Resistance and Difficulty' is notable for its exclusive recourse to classical, medieval and modern Catholic philosophers from Aristotle and Duns Scotus to the Franciscan scholar, Philotheus Boehner (1901–55) and the Aristotelian, John P. Anton (1920–2014). The key to understanding the delirious deletion, in its entirety, of the non-Catholic Western European philosophical tradition (and of British philosophy since Ockham) is the American phenomenologist, John Wild, whose graduate seminar at Harvard may have been the original context of Prynne's essay. What it purports to do, beginning with variations on the Aristotelian themes of 'substance... as the locus of processes' and 'the stone's hard palpable weight' as a criterion of reality, is to establish the ontological status of products of the imagination such as poems. What it actually does is to make an amazing identification of the 'embodied fusion of process with substance', as theorised by 'the phenomenological movement', with the Eucharistic body of Christ:

Just as for Marcel and Merleau-Ponty the existence of my body, as mine, bridges the gap between my consciousness and the world, so the substantial medium of the artist and the autonomy of his creation establish the priority of the world while at the same time making it accessible. In this way the ontology implicit in Hopkins's poetry draws much of its strength from a syntactical difficulty underpinned by etymological and phonetic resistance; the image of Christ's body as part of the natural order constantly reasserts the valid priority of substance.

Kazoo Dreamboats sustains the Aristotelian themes, its subtitle at once a reference to the Greek concept of being, 'τὸ ὄν' ('to on'), often translated as 'what there is'; and an attack on Wild's arch-antagonist, W.V.O. Quine, whose 1948 essay, 'On What There Is', determined the course of Harvard philosophy for generations. Let the name of Quine stand for everything excluded from 'Resistance and Difficulty', from empiricism to positivism – in Wild's terms, 'the Cartesian deformation of modern thought'. Descartes himself is succinctly dismissed by Prynne in a 1969 review as 'a minor mystagogue, the Willard Quine of Ultima Thule'! The meditations on the void of 'a proud heart crying out for self-being in struggle for joy', *Kazoo Dreamboats*, which reprises *The Oval Window* at every turn, offers 'Reference cues' to only a fraction of its unmistakable allusions; and the closing lines are crying out for the treatment:

To be this with sweet song and dance in the exit dream, sweet joy befall thee is by rotation been and gone into some world of light exchange, toiling and spinning and probably grateful, in this song.

One of these days, we shall have the Longman Annotated English Poets edition of Prynne's *Poems*. If I had Ernest Bevin's wartime powers, I would set these brilliant editors to work forthwith.

You Thought You'd Done

Derek Mahon, *Against the Clock*
(Gallery Press) £9.50

Reviewed by MAITREYABANDHU

Derek Mahon has set himself a hard act to follow. His poetry, as gathered in *New Collected Poems* (2011), warrants the widest possible readership. Muscular, impassioned and meticulously wrought, Mahon's best poems (and the hit rate, at least in the first three quarters of the *Collected*, is very high indeed) deserve to be read by anyone who turns to theatre, jazz, novels, biography and opera in order to help them live their lives. Anyone who takes Marilynne Robinson or George Saunders seriously as contemporary novelists, should take Mahon no less seriously as a contemporary poet. He is one of Ezra Pound's 'Good writers [...] who keep the language efficient. That is to say, keep it accurate, keep it clear.'

Because Mahon has set the bar higher than most of his contemporaries, the reader turns to *Against the Clock* – his first collection since the *New Collected* – with great expectations, and this is perhaps unfair. After the fire-spitting of 'New York Time', previously *The Hudson Letter* (1995), and 'Decadence', originally *The Yellow Book* (1997), *Against the Clock* lacks Mahon's incandescent rage. Nothing in the new collection is quite as accomplished as 'Courtyards in Delft', 'A Garage in Co. Cork', 'Inis Oírr', 'Afterlives' or those wonderful villanelles 'The Dawn Chorus' and 'Antarctica'. The unabashed 'A Birthday', celebrating his daughter's fortieth in *Against the Clock,* can't quite manage the sweet-and-sour brio of 'Yaddo, or A Month in the Country'. But then so much in the *New Collected* is so good that, not withstanding a late style as achieved as Wallace Stevens, a post-Collected collection is almost bound to disappoint.

Against the Clock begins with its title poem: 'Writing against the clock, the flying calendar / not to a regular but to a final deadline...' Mahon, at seventy-seven, remembers 'those who wrestled with language / until dementia or whatever struck'. Lamenting 'a naff culture not worth contributing to', the 'old faces' – Ovid, Dante, Yeats, Akhmatova – turn to him 'in disgust':

> You'd thought you'd done, the uneven output
> finished at last, but that wasn't the end,
> was it, since we're obliged to stick it out
> until the pen falls from the trembling hand;
> so just get on with it.

'Against the Clock' has many of the trademarks of Mahon's best work – rough-hewn metrical and rhyming form, undaunted content, affirmation of imagination, disgust with contemporary life – and yet the poem won't quite come off. It lights up but never flares. The collection as a whole feels like walking through a series of well-appointed rooms, each expressing the seriousness and taste of its owner, each worth pausing in, worth admiring, and yet it's as if the muse has just stepped out leaving only an after-trace of *eau de parfum*.

Nevertheless, there are strong poems. 'Jersey and Guernsey (after Hugo)' uses rhyming couplets to ignite a description of 'the demanding sea' and Hugo, an old man among schoolchildren, giving thanks: 'I live from day to day / peacefully in my own good time.' 'Rising Late', with its reference back to Hugo, is worthy of Mahon's best work:

> The vast sea-breath reminds us, even these days
> as even more oil and junk slosh in the waves,
> the future remains open to alternatives.

Combining many of Mahon's persistent themes – aubade, love of the natural world, climate change, revulsion for philistinism, the lives of exemplars (Plato in this case) – 'Rising Late', unlike the weaker poems in this collection, concludes with wonderful assurance:

> I would become, in the time left to me,
> the servant of a restored reality –
> chalks and ochres, birdsong, harbour lights,
> the longer days and the short summer nights.

Against the Clock closes with four of the book's strongest poems. 'A Dove in the House' recounts a childhood memory with Mahon's customary toughness and candour. 'A North Light' returns to the same council estate to commemorate the painter Basil Blackshaw 'who liked a drink / and the rough country life as it was once / before safety fascism assumed precedence.' 'Domestic Interior' pictures an ageing poet for whom only poetry, nature and domestic peace can hold a stay against 'deliberate ignorance and acquired odium.' The collection closes with 'Woodpigeons in the Grove' where unlovely woodpigeons, ignored by myth, stand in for the poet: 'self-contained to safety zones, / still dreaming of our once infinite horizons.'

Haunted by aging and death, by horizons – the sea a constant reminder of ephemerality but also of 'lost continents and nuclear waste' ('Horizons'), its roar never quite drowning 'the inane soundtrack/ of global capitalism' ('Cork in Old Photography') – at its best, *Against the Clock* is angry, aphoristic, tender and wonderfully made. It can surprise. When Mahon turns affectionate or amused as in 'A Birthday' or 'Being a Dog', the result is a deepening in our sense of his integrity: he is not a grumpy old man. Mahon's secular salvation of nature and art finds cogent expression at the close of 'Montaigne':

> I make nature my study as I grow old,
> unknowing to the last, in the known world.

But the feeling of Mahon *needing* to write creates a sense of strain. Mahon seems to recognise this. 'At the Window', a less achieved poem (by Mahon's standards) finishes with, 'I'm trying one more time / to find an opening in the stratosphere.'

In his important essay *Can Poetry Matter?*, the American poet and critic, Dana Gioia laments, 'the audience for poetry has declined into a subculture of specialists' and that 'outside the classroom [...] poets and the common reader are no longer on speaking terms.' He cites insipid reviewing as one of the causes and quotes Robert Bly: 'although more bad poetry is being published now than ever in American history, most of the reviews are positive.'

Mahon's strength in the face of so much poorly made poetry is formal rigour and disenchantment. He uses the forms of romanticism to spit in the eye of slobbishness and vanity, exemplifying, both in subject matter and formal skill, proper civility. Reading him, one feels in touch with an intellectual fire missing from so much modern verse. He is never writing for a poetry subculture, never fashionably obscure, sentimental or dubiously 'relevant'. His work contends with the best in contemporary fiction. Robinson's *Gilead* and Saunders's *Lincoln in the Bardo* show up contemporary poetry by out-doing it in prose. Many passages from Robinson's novels could be broken into verse in the manner Frost suggested to Edward Thomas, and Saunders's book could be read as a collection of inspired prose poems. So, *can poetry matter*? Mahon, especially in the *New Collected*, answers with proper subjects relevant to the concerned and intelligent reader, and form – rhyme, metre,

syntactic sophistication, 'memorable speech'.

But despite the urgency of his themes and his four-square form, there's a sense of Mahon not quite finding a unifying Idea. One can't help thinking that Mahon lacks 'religion'. Not in the conventional sense perhaps. Not God and his angels. But some transcending myth, an atmosphere of meaning or belief by the light of which – like the candle in George Eliot's image, unifying the apparently random scratches on a plate – content and form cohere into a subtler pattern. Robinson's Calvinism and Saunders's Tibetan Buddhism seem to give them a further reach. George Steiner in *Real Presences* concludes: 'What I affirm is the intuition that where God's presence is no longer a tenable supposition and where His absence is no longer a felt, indeed overwhelming weight, certain dimensions of thought and creativity are no longer attainable.' We are, as Steiner puts it, 'close neighbors to the unknown'. Mahon feels that 'unknown', it is one of themes of *Against the Clock,* and he is aware – how could he not be? – of God's absence, but he seems to have too readily accepted a thinking-man's 'scientific' secularism. And this can mean his 'salvation' of poetry and nature can't touch us as deeply as it should. What it can do, as in 'Working Conditions', is help us remember:

anything goes if it works, if it contribute
a howl or a whisper to the sum of wisdom.

Shaped around Wreckage

Jane Commane, *Assembly Lines* (Bloodaxe) £9.95

Reviewed by RACHEL MANN

When I grew up in the south Midlands of the 1970s, I spoke with an accent part-yokel, part-Brummie (Radio 4 listeners, think old-school *Archers* characters). As a teenager, I decided the only wise thing to do was drop it ASAP. If I wanted to get on, I decided I must take on the linguistic tropes and accent of the upper-middle class. Of course, in the past thirty years, such strategies have become somewhat frowned upon. Local accents and dialect are fashionable now, and even younger Royals like to flash a hint of Estuary English.

In poetry, the success of Liz Berry's *Black Country* arguably signalled a new shift towards the celebration of unfashionable, ugly English place and the language embedded in it. It is saturated in the dialect and accents of Dudley, Lye and Smethwick and, given how much the English midlands have been mocked, Berry's achievement was salutary.

Jane Commane's debut collection arguably relies on Berry's pioneering spadework. If it is not framed so much in dialect, it is defined by the midlands and specifically a place even less glamorous and more traduced than the Black Country: Coventry and its environs. Indeed, Commane playfully riffs on this in 'Coventry is', a list poem which suggests its 'always the bridesmaid and never the

bride, / is somewhere to be sent.' If this opening line relies on off-the-shelf language, Commane's power is found in barely suppressed anger about what has been lost, not only in human terms, but cultural infrastructure: 'preferring not to talk, tonight, of the masses buried / at London Road, the dead car plants, assembly lines.' This is, for all its gentle lyrical lines, a collection shaped around wreckage, of lives and of industry.

Assembly Lines relies, then, on an ambiguity between the lost industrial assembly lines of her midlands' youth and the assembled lines of those whose lives were destroyed by cruel economic policies. Perhaps this makes Commane's poetry sound like ranty polemic. Far from it, but the political is rarely far away. Even in her more elegiac moments, reaching back into childhood, she delivers lines like 'the sunset in the near that bleeds umber and gold / onto four walls once long with Thatcherite shadows.' The contrast between lyric smoothness and grand statement is bold, potentially jarring, but earns its keep.

'Assembly Lines' also gestures towards ideas about school and upbringing (think of the near-universal British experience of being forced to go to School Assembly once or twice a week). Childhood is present most notably in 'National Curriculum', which for English people of a certain age will always have connotations of Tory meddling in schools. A five-poem sequence, it makes some splendid linguistic gambits. In 'History', Commane suggests that, 'War is an onslaught of terrible mathematics', and in 'Geography', 'All you have taught us / is the story / of our own / destructions.' In 'Sciences' she balances a vision of throwing stones at the local boarding school with a wry sense of humour: 'An afternoon misspent in the study of gravity's trajectory; stones chipping the verandahs of the elite.'

For those who find Commane's brand of wry, lyric thoughtfulness and fury a little off-putting, 'Assembly Lines' finds much of its best territory when grappling with the terrain of language itself. The sequence 'UnWeather' – a play on 'unweder', the Old English for storm – is a stand-out that brings her politics (and specifically her bewilderment about the state of post-Brexit Britain) into conversation with the limits of what's sayable. If the latter is well-travelled territory, Commane's grip on contemporary matters steers her free from cliché. She suggests 'the little island tilts on its foundations, / threatens to tip you and the seasick dog loose / alone together on the burning edge as longshore drift / carries the crumbling biscuit nation off to sea.' It's pretty black-humoured stuff (suggestive of that famous line in Felicia Hemans's 'Casablanca'), funny without losing its linguistic grip. Perhaps, I'm still too caught up in the trauma of what happened in the 2016 Brexit Referendum, but I found Commane's claim that 'we need a new word for the theft / of something indefinable but definitely lifted' compelling. Surely she's right when she claims, 'Our tongues were made from / Sprechen, dicere, parler.'

Politics, trauma, 'the personal'. Each category – insofar as they are distinctive – have been mined relentlessly and often ineptly. Commane is bold and arguably brave to allow this trinity to make a kind of perichoretic dance through her writing. For those readers who (like Italian gangsters after revenge), prefer their politics and trauma 'served cold', I suspect 'Assembly Lines' will frustrate, at times. Pound famously suggested that poetry is news that remains new. It will be interesting to see how this collection settles over time. As a debut, it is engaging, timely and, for those of us of a certain age and background, laugh-out loud. The challenge for Commane from here will be to push her lyric gift harder and further, perhaps into new forms and registers. Her language may yet need to break apart for it to find fresh territories.

Digging Away

Elizabeth Parker, *In Her Shambles* (Poetry Wales) $9.99; Ari Banias, *Anybody* (W.W. Norton) $15.95

Reviewed by DAVID C. WARD

Looking up definitions of 'shambles' for this review, I find that it usually means 'wreckage' or 'mess' (an archaic meaning is the killing floor of a butcher's) but that there is a usage in which it is pridefully applied to gardens whose display is a seemingly artless cascade of surprising beauty. I like the idea of adopting Shambles as a term, like Folly or Ha Ha, for landscape gardening. I suspect Elizabeth Parker would too not least since turned into a verb, 'shambling', the term (rhyming with rambling) also means a kind of purposeless or awkward walk or gait. In gardening or poetry, then, 'shambles', as demonstrated by Parker, is an oxymoron, a seemingly accidental yet entirely purposeful aesthetic reconstruction of what she encounters. As we know, there is nothing natural about landscape. Rather it's how we design and arrange it: 'While he stayed shut, her throat bloomed / long-stemmed flowers / threading their colors through a breeze.' Or in 'Dry' a river is unclogged:

You sleeked my snarls of algae
brought a lush hiss to my throat
brown trout wafting their bodies.

It's not all blooms and flowage though as nature is as much muck and mire or decay; 'From Home to the Garden Centre The Forest of Dean' makes the forest viscous with industrial leavings: 'a forest still oozing iron, / bedrocks greased with ore.' Nature is dangerous, with a hint of the butcher shop's blood and offal:

Birds, shrews, mice
pried from the white portcullis

of the cat's teeth

Mostly, though, things are humid and mouldy: 'Our new spades prise a lid of dry soil / from loam riddled with red ants, rotten bulbs / last years hyacinths that failed to hatch / nipped and leached by microbes.' Or, from 'My Black Gardens': 'I relinquish my black gardens / matted kelp, ripe bladderwrack. / I lose skins'. Sloughing and relinquishing extends to people, relationships: 'A spider trails its tiny shadow / across the bathroom tiles. / Your heat is gone but there are scents'. 'Writing Him Out' is a nicely done 'breakup poem' about the ink running out (writing this poem presumably) and then rinsing the pen and flushing the watery residue: 'The plughole glugged up stained water / then swallowed him down for good.'

This flowage is amplified in several poems about running water and rivers. Poets like rivers because they're analogous to verse as well as to life. And Paker has several river poems, the best of which associates family members and friends with kinds of rivers:

My aunt's river grazes its banks
and widens
Rocks are loosed to salt her river
    [...]
My uncle's river remembers its monks
their nights rowing to secret mass
prows cutting water bonds
to rock chapels in the gorge

And:

This morning my river was high
green and urgent with rain
rushing light and leaves toward the estuary.

Rivers, though, are just a little too dramatic for Parker; the mood of 'Quiet Water' with its pipe 'bent up from mud / its leak snaking through outgrass and deadnettle / twitching each stem,' the field getting sodden, surprising the unwary. She favors a sense of decay, or decadence in poems that are astringently opulent. No more so than in 'Lizzie', her poem about the poems that Dante Gabriel Rossetti buried with his wife and then had exhumed:

> They plucked out his book
> with a bible and a worm
> leaves edged red
> bound in calfskin
> disinfectant reek
> when he unpeeled the rags.

Against this high drama (romantic but creepy!), Parker counterpoints the hum drum of modern wordprocessing; 'I spell-check / save as / rename / print / close / shut down.' Parker is being ironic or self-mocking here, if she uses a word processor, her sensibility is of the fountain pen – the piercing of the cartridge, the flow of ink, the sharpness of the nib.

Lurking behind this reference to a fountain pen is Seamus Heaney's famous injunction to his pen, 'I'll dig with it'. Dig, Parker does, into genealogy, history, and the land, freighting her poems with these connections.

Contrasting are the poems of Ari Banias whose title Anybody centers his subject not just on the possibility of connection but to the malleable defining of the body itself; the title could have had a question mark since the book is about finding oneself.

> The choices: cheating husband, vapid fag

checked-out corporate guy, self-centered evolved guy, sensitive yet inarticulate, predator, messiah, martyr, angry man…

It's very much a young person's book not least in its working through the self-definition of sexual identity. About fraught relations with his father: 'I know / I was afraid. Of him. And so. / I know I played alone / with dolls and that / we roughhoused, hard, like brothers.' Coming out aside, there's a fragility, even a naiviety, to these poems that works for a while but then gets cloying:

> The book I almost finished.
> The look I gave you
> while you weren't looking and now
> you'll never know the way I feel.

Dear Diary! There's an entire poem listing defunct and extant 'Gay Bars' in America; 'The Stonewall' isn't name checked which is too bad because it's not like Banias is the first person to go through these growing pains. A sense of history as well as a sense of irony wouldn't be amiss here. A little subjectivity goes a long way, especially these days when the 'coming of age' memoir / novel / poems has been done to excess. If you're going to do it you have to have a sense of style and Banias is just a little too in love with his own mopiness and self-dramatisation. There's an audience for this, of course, but having worked through this stage of his poetic autobiography it might be a good idea for Banias to go for a shamble.

Transformation

Cecilia Vicuña, *New and Selected Poems*, ed. by Rosa Alcalá (Kelsey Street Press) £26.95

Reviewed by LUKE ROBERTS

Cecilia Vicuña was born in Santiago in 1948, 'mixture of kings and idiots / nobility and commoner / shit and mud'. Her Grandfather, a civil rights lawyer, defended Pablo Neruda after the outlawing of the Communist Party in the 1940s, and as a child she read the other Chilean greats, Vicente Huidobro and Gabriela Mistral. By the mid-1960s she was part of the Latin American avant-garde, involved in poetry, conceptual art and performance.

Her publications have always been political. The first magazine she contributed to, *El Corno Emplumado*, was shut down by the authorities after it condemned the massacre of protestors in Mexico City in 1968. Her first book was destroyed by the Pinochet regime following the military coup in Chile in 1973. Vicuña, studying in England at the time, reworked the materials into her masterpiece, *Saborami*, a gesture of total defiance in the face of political disaster. In that book she describes a tactic that resonates throughout her career: *maximum fragility against maximum power*.

So any book by Vicuña seems precious, precarious, even this *New and Selected Poems* containing selections from ten different projects along with a generous sam-

pling of uncollected and unpublished material. It is a beautiful object, oversized, illustrated with drawings and photographs, and with facing-page translations throughout. Rosa Alcalá, who previously translated and edited Vicuña's performance texts *Spit Temple*, is a meticulous editor. Her selection presents the reader with a lifetime of work devoted to invention and reinvention, and to the causes of feminism, socialism, indigenous land rights and environmental justice.

In one of her earliest poems, Vicuña writes with irreverence and seriousness: 'I continue to feel I am / a shitty preacher: / I enlighten no one / more than me.' The casual reader might be tempted to agree. This is a difficult book, more unwieldy than *Saborami*, more oblique than *Spit Temple*. Vicuña's language compositions can sometimes read like preparatory documents, recording her searches for structure and form. During the 1980s, she travelled extensively in the Andes and developed a poetics influenced by scholarship into Mayan cosmology and indigenous textile work, including the *Quipu*, or knot languages. On occasion her assemblages of related citations and etymologies are too tantalising, like we're looking over the shoulder of the poet as she makes her discoveries.

But Vicuña is never solipsistic. Her work is profound in its commitment to social transformation, and with patience the surface difficulty gives way to a luminous generosity. The reader has to be nimble. If the poems sometimes break apart or threaten dissolution, it's because the work is exilic. Vicuña is prepared to use the materials to hand, to move between languages, to be contingent and temporary. As she writes in one of the highlights here, 'The Vicuña', employing the weaving metaphor central to her later creative imagination: 'The world / is a loose stitch // I've lost the thread // but I rag on.'

In her opening statement on poetics she writes: 'Poetry is a supreme affinity for the world's speech.' I take this to mean both the spoken languages of the people of the world and the speech of the earth itself. She describes at one point sleeping on a balcony as a teenager at the foot of El Plomo in Santiago, and how the stars and glaciers combined to produce words in her inner self. Later she writes that, 'As it breaks the glacier moans, releasing a cow's alveolar lament.' It's hard for the translation to parallel the Spanish, where the vowels are woven tightly in what Vicuña has called the 'melodic matrix' of the language. But Alcalá and the other translators have produced an English version which allows us to hear and to imagine these frequencies, this range.

For new readers, *Saborami* is still the most precise and accessible example of Vicuña's poetics. But this *New and Selected Poems* shows the scale for what it is. Major work, vital work – maximum fragility against maximum power.

Holding On

Michael O'Neill, *Return of the Gift*
(Arc) £9.99

Reviewed by DUNCAN WU

Michael O'Neill's fourth collection of poems, *Return of the Gift*, is based on the conceit that the best verse comes from the anteroom in which sins are shriven, burnt off, cast aside, before the soul makes its way to another place. It is only fitting that the gaze of such poetry be ill-disposed to flatter, unforgiving, cold. This is a sizeable collection of a hundred pages. There are many distinguished poems and it is difficult to know where to start. One of my favourites is 'Stalker':

'Cease and desist' more or less worked,
though malignancy still lurked
on the net, in the latest
misspelt post.

In the end, it's all grist;
the episode taught him one lesson,
giving, as it did, the lie
to those who deny
there is a place called purgatory,

but, were they to reply,
'In that case,
what was your sin?',
he'd be, in this instance, at a loss,

have to fall back on 'being born'.

The idea that the stalker, faced with the threat of legal action, might retreat into the relative safety of anonymous trolling, is transformed by that multisyllabic, guilt-ridden, shameless word 'malignancy' – and by 'lurked', the persistence of which finds an emphatic chime in 'worked'. Such resonances, more unsettling than the nuisance-value of an actual stalker, direct attention to the malignant, lurking cells which are the true subject of the poem. 'In the end, it's all grist', says O'Neill, harnessing idioms that fabricate the tone and inflection of the casual, spoken utterance – a softening-up exercise for what proves to be a score-settler. O'Neill's invocation of sin in relation to disease – particularly one with the power to persist – exemplifies a strategy of this collection: to use the grimly physical as the platform for a meditation on the spiritual.

O'Neill is a fine Romantic scholar. At a time when the academic world was awash with theorists, he published *The Human Mind's Imaginings: Conflict and Achievement in Shelley's Poetry* (1989). It was critical analysis written out of a profound love of the poetry. At the time it was found so regressive as to be excluded itself from serious consideration. Today O'Neill's scholarship is recognised, when much of what was published in that low, dishonest decade has vanished. He was capable of explaining that most closeted and self-involved of poets to the interested reader – not least for his clear-eyed engagement with the creative process. O'Neill's *Percy Bysshe Shelley: The Major Works* (2003, co-edited with Zachary Leader) provides the only portable, and least pretentious, paperback selection currently in print.

O'Neill's voice is unmistakably his own. His reading of others becomes incorporated into the creative process – which is why, at his most literary, O'Neill is most himself, whether adapting Baudelaire ('The Swan'), Leopardi ('To the Moon'), or Rilke ('Roman Fountain'). There is a moment in an ekphrastic sonnet inspired by a painting of Kandinsky, 'Landscape with Red Spots, No.2', which demonstrates this:

It cuts its course, our packed traghetto,
across the Grand Canal.
                    It'd cut its course,
your death, your quick, aortic death, across
the year, as though you'd somewhere new to go.

And yet I'd keep you for a short duration,
make-believe this room bequeathed by Peggy G,
shrine to the lilt and shimmer of Kandinsky,
held essences like yours through art's creation.

Spiritual yellow arcs, halos round red spots,
leave space for spidery hints that shape
a cemetery's outline – dark tints the clue.

But 'essences like yours'... the phrase rots;
even if your features crop up
everywhere, these brushstrokes can't recall you.

There is much that affects the reader: the way 'traghetto' echoes 'tragedy', the mimicking of the Styx by the Grand Canal, and a continual drip-drip-drip of detail that discloses, gradually, that this is an elegy (though of whom is never stated) – an elegy which, moreover, revolves round the eccentric but inspired notion that the dead are present at the creation of great works of art (derived, presumably, from Yeats's 'Long-Legged Fly'). With such precursors, the poem runs the risk of collapsing under their weight, but O'Neill's poetic language never strains against meaning: his is pure speech, not rhetoric. It is understated almost to the point of neglect, though none of the techniques used here is more downplayed than the manner in which O'Neill alludes to earlier writers.

Presented as self-quotation, 'essences like yours' has an unacknowledged literary source. It originates with the Chartist poet Thomas Cooper, whose *Purgatory of Suicides* (1845) asks:

> Is it decreed
> That essences like yours in afterstate
> Of absolute brutality prostrate
> Shall lie forever?

Cooper hopes the answer is 'no' – as, presumably, does O'Neill, even if the phrase 'rots'. As readers, we need know none of this, not least because O'Neill has thoroughly domesticated his diction to the point at which the resonances, even the context of the poem itself, seem to emerge naturally and unhesitatingly out of the thinking mind. The poet's craft, in other words, is to generate a sense of spontaneous utterance that conceals any sense of labour, and to render each thought, each word, native to the constructed self that is its speaker.

There are many poems of real moment in the book, among them the sequence 'From the Cancer Diary', about O'Neill's experience of the illness. A memorable part is entitled 'Mists':

> Mists spiriting up from the fells
> the sure and certain knowledge

they will continue to rise and catch
the gaze of others

after I'm no longer around
to steer the car towards

that imaginary vanishing point
I've had in mind for many years.

Or the leaves struggling free of branches
back in the old garden as every September

(it wouldn't surprise should a figure with pince-nez
turn up disconsolately pushing a pram)

girders and trucks banging out their dissonant music
from the nearby Garston container docks

my father in his chair in the Long Room,
reflecting on who knows what,

me lingering on beneath the wide sky

The self-elegising posture ('after I'm no longer around') is again familiar from Yeats – in this case, 'The Wild Swans at Coole' – but so elemental to the meditating self that there is nothing second-hand about it. It is as natural an emanation of the mind as the mists themselves. But the phrase here that has stayed with me since I first read this poem is 'that imaginary vanishing point / I've had in mind for many years'. The image (or non-image) is unexpected, the affect powerful. Why? Because it alludes quietly, unobtrusively, un-selfpityingly, to the unlearned habit of anticipating one's own demise – something almost impossible to talk about other than through metaphor. The power derives from O'Neill's acceptance of fallen human nature, and how it makes us desperate not to release our grasp on the world before of us.

Is Poetry Interesting?

Susan Gubernat, *The Zoo at Night* (University of Nebraska Press, 2017) $17.95; Stephen Burt, *Advice from the Lights* (Graywolf Press, 2017) £12.50

Reviewed by DAVID C. WARD

Is life all that interesting? I suppose some of the details can be but by and large the universal themes of the life cycle and making one's way in the world create broad patterns that are familiar to us all and whose ubiquity leaches them of interest. Coming of age? Fashioning identity? Forging relationships? Aging, mortality and dying? Yup. We've all been there! The template is pretty much the same for everyone so how to stand out in a crowd is the question. Narcissistic self-assertion seems to be in vogue at the moment; people lie a lot, 'curate' the presentation of their lives on Instagram and shout on Twitter. Since poets, presumably, are more sensitive and acute souls they have to find quieter ways to make life interesting to their readers so its style that counts. *The Zoo at Night* by Susan Gubernat and *Advice from the Lights* by Stephen Burts offer contrasting ways of getting through the life cycle.

Gubernat takes a familiar tack, writing loose, slightly prose-y, lines in which an ordinary situation or reflection takes a swerve into the unknown or the unsettling. Order is asserted as something wished for but seldom attained – from 'Spirit Level':

> What could we do but measure ourselves
> and be found wanting? The straight shall be made
> crooked. But I was a cock-eyed optimist
> for a time, convinced the air-bubble would hit

She has a series of poems on homey subjects – the spirit level or a feather duster and one about hand grinding beef or the operations of a clothesline, in which things go slightly off kilter or get ominous; the father metaphorically drowns in the spirit level's bubble. 'Vestibule' is a nicely judged small horror story, as its old fashioned beveled glass distorts the outer world so that 'From here, all the loose dogs on the street / appear rabid; the stranger keeps wanting/to get in, in.' In the series 'The Zoo at Night' that gives her her book title, Gubernat reverses this strategy, refusing to write about the tiger attack, 'forswearing the easy metaphor / of the unpredictable pent-up beast' to shift to the quiet agony of hand feeding one's aged mother: 'because the mere violence of your eye, / non-swipe of your paw, / were most unnatural, Mother.' It's in it's quiet moments that life is most upsetting: 'isn't it the child, / tight-lipped, refusing to fee, / who consternates the mother?' Gubernat always manages to surprise you, her relaxed lines and sudden shifts of point of view owe something to Frank O'Hara. She is always willing to be surprised herself, which is a good trait for anyone to have, no less than when she (a second generation American 'stumbling / into Culture') became a poet and feel in love 'headed, as I had been, for a different fate: suburban convent redolent of Lysol and bergamot, / with spouse or without.'

The instabilities in Stephen Burt's *Advice from the Lights* are more evident, even overt, both because he makes himself directly his subject and because of his own biography: Stephen Burt is now Stephanie Burt, they having transitioned in 2017. Gender fluidity runs through these poems, many of which refract the author's adolescence in the 1980s. 'The Cars' [remember them?] Greatest Hits' name checks 1980s culture to make the point that everything is pastiche or a fabrication; 'When everything is artificial / everything is equally sincere' and, 'If you synthesize your confidence, the more / you make up the less you have to fear.' As Wile E. Coyote well knows, it's looking down that kills you.

Stylistically, Stephen/Stephanie uses jittery lines and jump cuts from topic to topic to foreground his adolescent indeterminacy. He captures the shaky put-on confidence of kids – the serious, sensitive or artistic ones

anyway – trying out roles and creating their own spaces. He's self aware; his favorite teacher admonishes him for his constant chatter in class and without: 'we'd like you to think // about what might be interesting to your friends, // not just about what's interesting to you.' Lesson learned? Kind of. Some poems are just not that interesting: I am sad / when I pad / my bra, or my imagined training bra.' The sociology of 'Mean Girls' is not particularly compelling: 'We will grow up to study your mistakes / As means of navigation.' 'After Callimachus' does better on the evolution, not so much into identity or adulthood but into poetry:

> Why do I write? Experience
>   and scientific evidence agree:
> an otherwise intolerable load
>   of shame decreases by up to six percent
> if told to even a temporary companion

and ends with a nice image of fear diminishing 'whenever secrets/are no longer secrets and enter the common/ atmosphere, even as birdsong, even in code.' Burt is willing to show how he is working his way through to learning to write in code. The subjects in this evolution are not always that compelling – and Burt can be just a little too girlish and camp – but he gets what the problem is: how to make dailiness interesting or compelling. The last several poems in *Advice from the Lights* take a slightly more traditional approach to writing, stating a subject and then examining it without foregrounding the autobiography of the speaker. There are even nature poems which is a bit unexpected and the last poem, 'White Lobelia' ends with an image to build on:

> We tell ourselves
> and one another that if you listen
> with sufficient
> generosity, you will be able
> to hear our distinctive and natural sound.

Structure Becoming Sentience

Chris McCabe, *The Triumph of Cancer* (Penned in the Margins) £9.99

Reviewed by DOMINIC LEONARD

In his fifth book of poetry, *The Triumph of Cancer*, Chris McCabe explores cancer in its physical intricacies down to an atomic level, as well as in its metaphorical possibilities socially and politically. As the poet reminds us, it only takes one cancerous cell for malignancy to 'spread... sideways out, like fingers, outwards', and in the collection this much is true for victims of cancer as well as for anybody trying to navigate a world caught up in self-perpetuating chaos.

McCabe is at his strongest in moving elegies for his father, particularly the opening poem 'Crab', which ties the etymology of 'carcinogen' to the memory of a family

holiday, and 'Cancer', which flits between images and time-frames along an abstract Tube journey. As the speaker rides through tunnels, as if through the veins of a body in the process of self-sabotage, the poet balances the simplicity of a regular commute – 'I take cash from the ATM, switch to the DLR & check my texts' – with the heavy conceptual weight of the topic undertaken: 'And the tube started. To say she alighted would simplify how heavy / it feels to move forward alone, away from the dance of endorphins.' T. S. Eliot's influence is felt in the poem, from its epigraph to its Prufrockian reflections and the narrator's tour through half-deserted platforms, and imagery reminiscent of *Four Quartets* ('In my commute begins / the death in my prime'). The mind, in this poem, is unable to stay still when forced to dwell with something so incomprehensible. McCabe is also well-suited to the metaphysical mode he often writes in; a poem comparing the spreading of cancer cells to snooker balls is unexpectedly moving, as is a tribute to David Bowie's 'one liver'.

But although *The Triumph of Cancer* is conceptually strong and has moments of excellence (mostly in the first half), it feels overlong and unfocused. Responses to Blake, Donne and Hopkins, and a particularly toe-curling poem on the importance of libraries that reads like a half-baked Laureate commission ('Noise in the library is the equivalent to a streaker at a funeral') left me feeling cold. The book's project, to write the (specifically male) body as a site of self-inflicting violence, ends up coming across as overwrought when weighed down by poems whose inclusion left me confused and frustrated. In the collection's most promising moments there is a kind of curated bafflement in the face of bodily and global violence, and how to navigate the two using cancer as a lodestone – but many of the poems wander from this framework, or the efforts are unsuccessful.

Within *The Triumph of Cancer* is a superb pamphlet – I have Liz Berry's recent *The Republic of Motherhood* in mind as an example of what the shorter form could have done for this project – but unfortunately, the collection as it stands does not reach the level of the poet's previous work.

Diction and Contradiction

Keith Bosley, *The Wedding Guest: Selected Poems*, edited by Owen Lowery and Anthony Rudolf, (Shoestring Press) £12

Reviewed by HILARY DAVIES

There is a poignancy about the publication of this volume of Keith Bosley's selected verse. It is the first retrospective of his work, an attempt to give a sense of the range of a poet who had gained recognition primarily for his outstanding verse translations from the Finnish, in particular their national epic, *The Kalevela*. Bosley, who had been in ill health for some time, held the volume in his hands but died within a few months of the collection appearing, so an opportunity to assess the body of his own poetry is timely.

Anthony Rudolf, in his preface, reminds us that those who are highly regarded for their translations often find their own poetry neglected, and this is certainly the case with Bosley.

What emerges from this volume is a man of contradictions: he was rooted in the landscapes of Berkshire, documenting both its idyllic pastoral and the suburban, railway-driven, car-driven creep of the nineteenth and twentieth centuries. Yet he voyaged far out in his imagination, both as a gifted linguist and translator and also, for many years, as one of the BBC *World Service*'s most well-known and loved presenters. He was an accomplished musician and local church organist, whose marriage to the Finnish harpist, Satu Salo, led to a decades-long engagement with the imaginative world of a country far to the north and east and far, far wilder than the gentle banks of the Thames. Bosley was equally at home in French, which he read at university and his versions from this language are as assured as his Finnish: he was a poet with a particularly heightened sense of the richness of other cultures and the dense metaphorical possibilities of words.

His own language, however, is usually spare, even sparse, pared down to a minimum to convey the apparently humdrum existences of those amongst whom he lived: evacuees from the Blitz, his father mending shoes, allotment tenders. But there is a persistent presence of those who come from more exotic, and indeed sinister places, people who have run mad because of what they have seen. This surfaces in a major way in the title poem which evokes the hellish experiences of a Latvian refugee from the Nazis. But this raises a problem that always accompanies attempts to write about the catastrophe that befell specifically Europe during the Second World War, without actually having experienced it at first hand (Bosley was a boy in England at the time), and he does not escape this. He eschews any kind of poetic flourish as inappropriate to the recitation of horror, keeping to a deadpan narrative; but dry language in itself does not guarantee poetic effectiveness. Ironically, there is not enough linguistic fashioning to make the poem really succeed. And a language '*qui rase la prose*' dominates a lot of the selection.

For this reviewer, it is the love poems to his wife that marry language and feeling with most felicity; ecstasy is bodied forth by lyricism. 'Fairy Tale with Harp' deftly avoids the sentimentality the title might suggest to present us with the privileged moment when two people fall unexpectedly and completely in love. The man makes a clumsy attempt at overture upon the harp that unites them, and she responds, magnificently, 'She seized the instrument: / on its seven pedals / she trod, setting the pitch / flat, natural or sharp/ for each step of the scale / across the whole body's/ range, so that when she swept / the strings there was music / and they were together'.

Shakin' All Over

John James, *Sarments: New and Selected Poems*; Barry MacSweeney, *Desire Lines: Unselected Poems 1966–2000* (both Shearsman)

Reviewed by JOHN MUCKLE

John James, who has died recently, lived just long enough to see this book into print, and to read from it, at a whisper, at a launch event at Swedenborg Hall, Bloomsbury. This whispered delivery, from a skeletal beanpole of a man who still managed to look stylish in a ritually self-conscious working-class art-rocker sort of way, has found its way into my reading of his poetry, early and late, in this crisply edited self-summary of his long career as an O'Hara-poet of aestheticised leftism: a French-dwelling gallerygoers catalogue of *rendez-vous* with numbers of beautiful women under the watchful, prurient eyes of Baudelaire and Bataille, all of it studied, turned inside out and held – forever – in poems that seem to aspire to the monumental stillness and gravity of

Mallarmé looking at one of Mery's fans. It might be said that he always risked absurdity, hanging on to rock'n'roll for longer than was seemly, stuck semi-fast to working-class allegiances and elderly Stalinist boozers; but from this pleasing, elegant redux of his poetry such elements have been purged in favour of sweet memories, whispered reminiscence and the rituals of pleasure: pouring wine, beginning a conversation, recalling people who shared this life. But wait! Is that all? There is very often something a little sardonic about these poems, which discreetly withhold much personal detail. Confessional he is not. It is often the moment of setting out that is offered: the beginnings of an encounter, or the overall mood of an evening, the essence of a memory of promise. Although there is little of the mess of what happened, there is the faint self-mockery of somebody who knows just what he is avoiding.

> it's Saturday & the Bohemian proletariat
> gather at The Empress at six thirty sharp
> the talk is of a Portuguese departure
>
> as the blackbird sings
> Virilio Virilio
>   ('Romsey, Take 2', p. 21)

A 'sarment' is a thin stem or runner that forms a new plant in 'Recollection Ode: Les Sarments' they are perhaps the threads of memory than run between Wordsworthian spots in time in rural France, Cambridge, Bristol and elsewhere, and in these Romsey poems a series of tendrils strike out from a much earlier poem, 'Bye Bye Blackbird', in which 'sprats & opals' are dreamed of in Brightlingsea, Essex (in the company of fellow poet Douglas Oliver), and here meet with Paul Virilio, the French philosopher of speedy departures, and in the same sequence, Amélie Mauresmo, the French tennis star, thoughts of whom banish the blackbird of depression as surely as 'a latch-lifter / in the tavern / before dinner'.

As if in apology for his swerving towards such distractions, this selected poems opens with an ill-tempered frontal assault on the 'baleful pornographic dance' of modern celebrity culture, empty comforts and a swift retrospect of the post-war 'never had it so good' period of which James and his poetic contemporaries were resisters, counterposing friendship and authentic connection to a public-political language seen as empty, a consumerism degrading to the people and a lie. James, as though he feared that the expression of a wider politics edged him into speaking falsely, has culled much of this work, but here he speaks out: 'I reach towards the poetry of kindred / where we speak in our work as we seldom do otherwise' ('Poem Beginning with a Line of Andrew Crozier', p. 61). The problem being that one's sense of 'kindred' or 'kind' (these senses are borrowed from his friend Douglas Oliver) may not be as encompassing or authoritative as one had wished, or hoped for. This is an excellent introduction to his poetry, attuned to its times.

Barry MacSweeney didn't live to make a final judicious rearrangement of his greatest hits, but the chequered publishing history of his work has been posthumously rectified by a generous selected poems from Bloodaxe, and now this large gathering of 'unselected' poems, thoughtfully edited and introduced by Luke Roberts. It is in effect half of MacSweeney's collected poems, although by no means complete or exhaustive, Roberts tells us. I remember hearing him read from a journalistic novel called, I think, something like *Muckraker*, and being impressed by its precise tone, nuances of speech and powers of observation. Presumably it's still nestling in the archives at Newcastle University; but almost anything by MacSweeney could be spellbinding in delivery where that mixture of barely controlled passion and detached intelligence was most evidently present.

On the page it's a slightly different story – the repeated whiplash of his spiky phrasemaking neologism (which is unique and wonderful!) stops, after a while, producing any delicious tingling sensations and becomes simply sore. Printing the unselected half of books works especially well when they contain the boy-like cocky lyricism of his early collections, *The Boy from the Green Cabaret Tells of His Mother* and *Our Mutual Scarlet Boulevard*, but is less satisfying in the sometimes hectoring late work, powerful though it can be. In between is unseen or fugitively published poetry, much of it impressive, including his poems for and with Elaine Randell, which are touching and show a more, tender, loving side. 'Soft Hail', hitherto unpublished, seems to return to these in feeling, and reminded me of the pained negotiations between the newlywed Brangwens in D.H. Lawrence's *The Rainbow*, with its notations of rural Northern landscape and an angry acceptance of cleavage between a man and a woman.

> She
> returned –
> curlew
> whooping
> over gorse.
> The wind blew.
> He faced
> the gale.
> Plovers rose
> and resettled
> and he humped
> his bag of stones
> door to door.
> ('Soft Hail', p 205)

A real highlight of *Desire Lines* is the complete text of *Black Torch* (1978), published on the brink of Thatcherism, a book-length poem inspired by the miners' strikes of 1972 and 1974. This poem is a projectivist vortex composed of glimpses of mining history and struggle harking back to the 1830s, taking in the May '68 événements in Paris, Newcastle City Council corruption scandals, poignant snippets of the harsh lives of nineteenth century child miners, woven through with glimpses of the ranter schools and other initiatives which aimed to turn mining communities into a self-defining political force. The realities of dependence on rapacious owners and fluctuating markets are also apparent in this moving collage work, whose excavation here reveals a record of dashed hopes that glitters darkly with found diamonds and pearls.

> black quilts
>   black torch

```
      salt tears standing
    she fair flower
        water swam with speed
loup for rough hills
        perilous Farnes
star-haunted Ida
        presenting fire
not drowsing south
        storm & glade music
storm is lord
        & midnight evil-starred
breaking in foam
    Coquet Font & Tyne
    ('Melrose to South Shields', p. 163)
```

Moments of lyric reprieve like this lift the poem and

balance out the dialect voices of miners, reminding us of the perceived 'natural' force of a complex cultural and political history, a Laurentian sense of humans in a breathing landscape that has both depth and quickness. But the seventies strikes were after all victories. The anger and political despair of MacSweeney's later poetry is a direct response to the final defeat of 1984–85, and therefore this poem is crucial to understanding his work in context – an explanation at least for what might otherwise appear to be incoherent, unanchored rage about his own predicament as a poet. MacSweeney was an unapologetic myth-maker, a personal poet whose gallows humour turns late poems like 'I Am Lucifer' and his versions of Apollinaire into an extreme kind of comedy, and perhaps he was best as a deliquescent dandy on his last legs. In this work, however, he articulates a larger myth.

Creatures Fiercely Made

Shara Lessley, *The Explosive Expert's Wife* (U. of Wisconsin Press) £13.50; Danielle Boodoo-Fortuné, *Doe Songs* (Peepal Tree Press) £8.99; Jennifer Elise Foerster, *Bright Raft in the Afterweather* (U. of Arizona Press) £16.50

Reviewed by YVONNE REDDICK

Shara Lessley's latest collection takes us to Jordan, viewed through the eyes of an expatriate woman from the USA. The book gets off to a strong start with a poem about the Middle East's first all-female demining team:

> Women go down on their knees
> hovering above a mapwork of metalwork, brushing
> dust from cluster bombs like ash from flatbread.

The line break after the first line creates an accomplished sleight of hand: you think this is a poem about prayer, or sex, but no! Lessley's poetry continues to surprise: the scorpions are far less dangerous than the 'dragons' teeth' mines; Queen Noor is from the Midwest. The poet deftly captures cultural differences throughout the collection – Arabic has a phrase for 'the static of snow-crust forming / white camellias of ice', but the local Jordanian dialect has no word for 'Miss'.

Yet one of the book's greatest strengths is the delicate way it finds common ground across cultures. 'My passport reads *Shara*, a Nabatean god // Am I more or less American in Amman?' the poet wonders in 'Ex-pat Ghazal'. The explosive expert's wife recurs in all three sections of the collection (first packing clean underwear for her husband's trip to Kabul, and later witnessing him testing mines in a Department of Defense range). Some of the collection's most intriguing poems look at America with fresh eyes: 'The Bath Massacre, 1927' examines America's first school bombing, while 'The Clinic Bomb-

er's Mother' is a companion piece to the Jordan-focused 'The Accused Terrorist's Wife'. Poetic forms range from a loose ghazal to the airy, open free verse in 'Arab Spring' series. The result is a book that is formally diverse, but whole and balanced in theme. Personal, political and distinctive, this is a strong volume.

'See how I am fiercely made', says the daughter in Danielle Boodoo-Fortuné's 'Dream of my Daughter as a Fawn'. In this distinctive first book by the Trinidadian poet, mythic transformations illuminate a complex web of human relationships. Told in sparse free verse where even a labouring mother animal has 'third and fourth sets of teeth', the imagery is raw and powerful. Shape-shifting informs the prize-winning poem 'Portrait of my Father as a Grouper', and the astonishing poem of pregnancy and miraculous healing, 'Boa Gravida':

> I am the great mother boa
> turning the soft egg of the world
> beneath my ribs. I will tear myself in two
> and heal before morning.

This collection is heir to Pascale Petit's poetry of shamanic transformation, but its literary midwife might be Derek Walcott's Ma Kilman. Boodoo-Fortuné's rich vocabulary of cornbirds, guyaba juice and bellbirds immerses us in Trinidadian landscapes, while avoiding cliché. Readers of Caribbean poetry in English already have a luscious menu of star-apples, breadfruit and ackee to choose from; it is a welcome change that Boodoo-Fortuné uses these images to evoke an unsettling wildness. Litany and devotional literature – the novena, the book of hours – lend a religious gravitas to powerful sequences about childbirth and the deaths of loved ones. Elsewhere, as in the extraordinary poem 'Jaguar Mary, María Lionza', the mother of wild things is barely Christianised. This poem's tall spine of verse, with what looks like a pelvis at its base, mirrors the form of Alejandro Colina's famous statue of Jaguar Mary in Venezuela. Most of the shape-poems deftly challenge a unified conception of the lyric 'self', although occasionally, the purpose of the experimental form is not always entirely clear – 'Waiting' is a case in point. Overall, though, this is a fascinating collection, recommended for readers who like their poetry with teeth, claws and a dash of surrealism.

Jennifer Elise Foerster's *Bright Raft in the Afterweather* tackles the weighty theme of climate change in fresh and surprising ways. The collection opens with an old Mvskoke woman who narrates what looks like a creation-myth:

> A star, the sun, was born in the dark.
> Salt leached from rocks.
> The ocean rusted.

However, it quickly becomes clear that these poems are tales of apocalypse, not genesis. This is a world in which, 'The continent is dismantling' and the speaker in 'Canyon' must find 'a raft for the coming storm'. There are moments of breathtaking natural beauty: 'gold-headed thistles igniting the apse', 'drifting monuments / crash and calve'. However, these are always used to throw environmental damage into relief – 'On the plastic raft / I clutch my trash'. With the ghostly presence of a 'red-ochered Beothuk', Foerster provides a sombre reminder of the persecution of Native Americans – the erosion of pre-capitalist ways of life contributing to environmental damage.

The poems are slender in shape, frequently incorporating blank space. Foerster often uses a form that weaves across the page: 'Land Art' does this to echo the movement of grasses. 'Catch' has a meandering shape that masterfully captures movement in a fishing scene, but it is in this poem that Foerster's fluid human and animal subjects risk confusing readers and giving them the slip.

'Lost Coast' brings the collection to a crescendo, with portents of drowned cities. The book ends with an accomplished picture of a world that ends not with a bang, but a snowstorm:

> That the world would end in snow,
> an old woman walking alone,
> empty birdcage strapped to her back.

These poems have a lyrical finesse and technical control that is disappointingly rare in some recent work about environmental crisis. (Juliana Spahr and Joshua Clover's '#Misanthropocene' and Craig Santos Perez's 'Halloween in the Anthropocene' are good examples of poetic fighting talk that nevertheless risks glibness.) Foerster's image of a lone woman survivor looking for her crow is a resonant way to bring this powerful collection to a close.

SOME MORE CONTRIBUTORS

G. C. Waldrep is the author most recently of *feast gently* (Tupelo, 2018) and the long poem *Testament* (BOA Editions, 2015). He lives in Lewisburg, Pa., where he teaches at Bucknell University and edits the journal *West Branch*. From 2007 to 2018 he served as editor-at-large for *The K.* **Nina Iskrenko** (1951–1995) was an influential poet of the Moscow New Wave in the 1980s, and a member of the unofficial Moscow club Poetry. Following the putsch in 1991 she became a member of the Russian Writers' Union. She published three books of poetry in 1991, and her work appeared in many journals. In 1995 she received the Yeltsin Award for her poetry. She died of cancer aged forty-three. **Anne Gutt** is a poet and translator. She was awarded the Gabo Prize for Literary Translation for her translations of poems by Ganna Shevchenko. **André Naffis-Sahely** is the author of *The Promised Land: Poems from Itinerant Life* (Penguin, 2017). His translations include over twenty titles of poetry, fiction and nonfiction. He is the poetry editor of *Ambit* magazine. **Karen Leeder** is Professor of Modern German Literature and Fellow and Tutor in German at New College, Oxford. Her work has won the Schlegel Tieck prize, the Stephen Spender prize anthe John Frederik Nims Memorial Prize for Translation 2017. **Rachel Mann** is an Anglican priest and writer. Author of five books, a selection of her poems is included in Carcanet's *New Poetries VII*. **Sasha Dugdale** is a poet and translator and former editor of *MPiT*. She is currently working on translations of Maria Stepanova's poems for publication in 2019.

COLOPHON

Editors
Michael Schmidt (General)
Andrew Latimer (Deputy)

Editorial address
The Editors at the address on the right. Manuscripts cannot be returned unless accompanied by a stamped addressed envelope or international reply coupon.

Trade distributors
NBN International
10 Thornbury Road
Plymouth PL6 7PP, UK
orders@nbninternational.com

Design
Luke Allan
Typeset by Andrew Latimer in Arnhem Pro.

Represented by
Compass IPS Ltd
Great West House
Great West Road, Brentford
TW8 9DF, UK
sales@compass-ips.london

Copyright
© 2019 Poetry Nation Review
All rights reserved
ISBN 978-1-78410-156-5
ISSN 0144-7076

Subscriptions (6 issues)
INDIVIDUALS (print and digital): £39.50; abroad £49
INSTITUTIONS (print only): £76; abroad £90
INSTITUTIONS (digital): subscriptions from Exact Editions (https://shop.exacteditions.com/gb/pn-review)
to: *PN Review*, Alliance House, 30 Cross Street, Manchester M2 7AQ, UK

Supported by

Supported using public funding by
ARTS COUNCIL ENGLAND